ARABIC

Verbs

& Essentials of Grammar

Second Edition

Jane Wightwick, Mahmoud Gaatar

Mc
Graw
Hill

New York Chicago San Francisco Lisbon London Madrid Mexico City
Milan New Delhi San Juan Seoul Singapore Sydney Toronto

2 3 4 5 6 7 8 9 10 11 12 13 14 15 16 17 18 19   CUS/CUS   0 9

ISBN 978-0-07-149805-0
MHID   0-07-149805-2

McGraw-Hill books are available at special quantity discounts to use as premiums and sales promotions, or for use in corporate training programs. For more information, please write to the Director of Special Sales, Professional Publishing, McGraw-Hill, Two Penn Plaza, New York, NY 10121-2298. Or contact your local bookstore.

This book is printed on acid-free paper.

Contents

Part Two: *Arabic Essentials of Grammar*

Introduction

This book is intended for beginning and intermediate learners of Arabic. You could be studying in a group or by yourself. Either way, you should find this book an essential and accessible introduction to Arabic verbs and grammar and a helpful on-going reference.

We are assuming a basic knowledge of the Arabic script as it is not possible to teach this skill within the parameters of this guide. However, to help you we have also included transliteration throughout, using a simplified system (see Appendix (i), page 124).

Arabic Verbs and the Essentials of Grammar aims to make Arabic grammar more understandable by presenting it in an accessible style. This guide covers most of what you will need to know about Arabic verbs during your study of modern Arabic, and also provides a useful summary of the main grammar points.

This is a study aid rather than a course. However, there is progression in the two main parts of the book, or you can simply dip in to brush up on a particular area.

Verb Index

This second edition also includes a comprehensive *Verb Index* listing 400 high-frequency Arabic Verbs (including all those in this book). The index will enable you to look up individual verbs in Arabic or English alphabetical order and find out their pronunciation, root letters and type. You will then be able to reference them to the relevant sections in this book. Not only this, you will also gain a better insight into how the Arabic verbal system works in general, and so be able to use other advanced dictionaries and references more effectively.

We hope you find this book a useful tool in your study of Arabic.

1 The Arabic root system

The key to understanding how Arabic grammar works is in its system of roots. Once you understand how roots work, you can start to identify which are the root letters of a word and understand the patterns they produce. You will then be able to form the different structures following the patterns and use your knowledge to pronounce words correctly and to guess at the meaning of vocabulary.

We can begin by looking at some English words:

necessary
unnecessary
necessitate
necessarily
necessity

As a speaker of English, you can see that these words are connected in meaning. You see the combination of letters "necess" and you know that this word is connected with the meaning of "needing." You can recognize the extra letters on the beginning and end of the word as additional to the meaning: *un-* meaning "not"; the ending *-ity* showing that the word is a noun; *-ly* that it is an adverb, etc.

Now look at these Arabic words:

كتب (*kataba*) he wrote
كتاب (*kitaab*) book
مكتب (*maktab*) office
يكتب (*yaktub*) he writes
كاتب (*kaatib*) writer

Can you spot the three Arabic letters that appear in each of the words on the previous page? You should be able to see that these letters appear in all the words:

    1. ك *(kaaf)*   2. ت *(taa')*   3. ب *(baa')*

(Look at *Appendix (i)* if you need to remind yourself of the Arabic alphabet.)

Notice that the letters appear in the same order in all of the words: the *kaaf* comes first, then the *taa'*, and finally the *baa'*. These three letters, in this order, are the root.

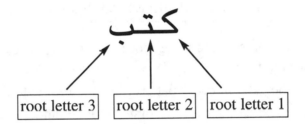

root letter 3   root letter 2   root letter 1

Look back at the previous page again and see if you can spot these three root letters in all the words. Notice that sometimes there are other letters as well as the root letters, but the root letters will always appear in the same sequence.

The root sequence we have looked at (*kaaf, taa', baa'*) is connected with the meaning of "writing." Whenever you see a word with this root, it probably has something to do with writing. The root letters mushroom into many different possible words. For example, when the root letters are put into a particular pattern with the letter *miim* (م) at the front, the meaning becomes "a place of writing," or "a desk/an office":

مكتب *(maktab)*

The vast majority of Arabic words contain three root letters, as in the example above. Much of Arabic grammar is concerned with manipulating the three root letters into different patterns. If you look back at the English words on the first page of this chapter, you will see that most of the changes take place at the beginning and the end of the word, leaving the core untouched. Arabic, on the other hand, adds letters, or combinations of letters, <u>between</u> the root letters, as well as on the beginning and end. Look at the word for "book" (*kitaab*):

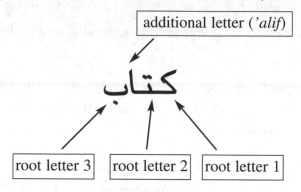

As a symbol to represent the three root letters of any word, Arabic grammar uses the letters فعل (f/ع/l). So the word for "office" – مَكْتَب (*maktab*) – is the مَفْعَل (*mafعal*) pattern; i.e., the root letters have ma (مَ) before them, a *sukuun* (ْ) over the first root letter and a *fatHa* (َ) over the second root letter. In the same way, the word كتابة (*kitaaba*) would be the فعالة (*fiعaala*) pattern, كُتُب (*kutub*) would be the فُعُل (*fuعul*) pattern, etc. In the first chapters of the book, we have tried to also use other common words to illustrate the patterns. However, later we have introduced more examples using فعل, since this is the convention understood most widely by both native speakers and Arabists.

You will find the root system very helpful once you have understood the concept and been introduced to some of the more common patterns. Native Arabic speakers have an instinctive understanding of how their language works, but as a learner you will need to approach it more methodically. Soon you will begin to see the pattern and the shape of words, and the structure of the language will start to become apparent.

Using a dictionary

It is worth adding a note about how to use an Arabic dictionary. It is possible to put Arabic in strict alphabetical order as we do in English, and this is becoming more common in the age of computerized alphabetization (see page 124 for the order of the Arabic letters). However, the most widely used dictionary for learners (*A Dictionary of Modern Written Arabic,* Hans Wehr) uses a system based on the *root* letters of the word. This means all words with the same root letters are grouped together. You will need to try and figure out the root letters of a word before you can look it up in the dictionary. Here is an example, showing the root كتب (*katab*):

كتب *kataba u* (*katb*, كتبة *kitba*, كتابة *kitāba*) to write, pen, write down in writing, note down, enter, record, book, register (ه s.th.); to compose, draw up, indite, draft (ه s.th.); to bequeath, make over by will (ل ه s.th. to s.o.); to prescribe (على ه s.th. to s.o.); to foreordain, destine (ل or على ه s.th. to s.o.; of God); pass. *kutiba* to be fated, be foreordained, be destined (ل to s.o.) | كتب على نفسه ان to be firmly resolved to ..., make it one's duty to ...; كتب عنه to write from s.o.'s dictation; كتب كتابه (*kitābahū*) to draw up the marriage contract for s.o., marry s.o. (على to) II to make (ه s.o.) write (ه s.th.); to form or deploy in squadrons (ه troops) III to keep up a correspondence, exchange letters, correspond (ه with s.o.) IV to dictate (ه ه to s.o. s.th.), make write (ه s.th.) VI to write to each exchange letters, keep up a correspondence VII to subscribe VIII to write (ه s.th.); to copy (ه s.th.), make a copy (ه of s.th.); to enter one's name; to subscribe (ل for); to contribute, subscribe (ل ب money to); to be entered, be recorded, be registered X to ask (ه s.o.) to write (ه s.th.); to dictate (ه ه to s.o. s.th.), make (ه s.o.) write (ه s.th.); to have a copy made (ه by s.o.)

كتاب *kitāb* pl. كتب *kutub* piece of writing, record, paper; letter, note, message; document, deed; contract (esp. marriage contract); book; الكتاب the Koran; the Bible | اهل الكتاب *ahl al-k.* the people of the Book, the adherents of a revealed religion, the kitabis, i.e., Christians and Jews; كتاب الزواج *k. az-zawāj* marriage contract; كتاب الطلاق *k. aṭ-ṭalāq* bill of divorce; كتاب تعليمى (*taʿlīmī*) textbook; كتاب الاعتماد credentials (dipl.); دار الكتب library

كتبي *kutubī* pl. -ya bookseller, bookdealer

كتابخانة *kitābḵāna* and كتبخانة *kutubḵāna* library; bookstore

كتاب *kuttāb* pl. كتاتيب *katātīb²* kuttab, Koran school (lowest elementary school)

كتيب *kutayyib* booklet

كتابة *kitāba* (act or practice of) writing; art of writing, penmanship; system of writing, script; inscription; writing, legend; placard, poster; piece of writing, record, paper; secretariat; written amulet, charm; pl. كتابات writings, essays; كتابة *kitābatan* in writing | بالكتابة written; بدون كتابة *bi-dūn k.* unwritten, oral; blank; كتابة التاريخ historiography, historical writing; كتابة الدولة *k. ad-daula* (Maḡr.) secretariat of state; كتابة عامة (ʿāmma) secretariat general; اسم الكتابة *ism al-k.* pen name, nom de plume; آلة الكتابة typewriter; لغة الكتابة *luḡat al-k.* literary language; ورق الكتابة *waraq al-k.* writing paper

كتابي *kitābī* written, in writing; clerical; literary; scriptural, relating to the revealed Scriptures (Koran, Bible); kitabi, adherent of a revealed religion; the written part (of an examination) | اسلوب (*uslūb*) literary style; غلطة كتابية (*ḡalṭa*) slip of the pen, clerical error; اعمال كتابية clerical work, office work, desk work; الكمال الكتابي (*kamāl*) literary perfection; لغة كتابية (*luḡa*) literary language; موظف كتابي (*muwaẓẓaf*) clerk, clerical worker (of a government office)

كتيبة *katība* pl. كتائب *katāʾib²* squadron; cavalry detachment; (Eg. 1939) battalion, (Ir. after 1922) regiment, (later) battalion, (Syr.) battalion of armored, cavalry, or motorized, units (mil.); (piece of) writing, record, paper, document; written amulet

مكتب *maktab* pl. مكاتب *makātib²* office; bureau; business office; study; school, elementary school; department, agency,

The Arabic–English verb index on pages 128–143 of this book is arranged in strict alphabetical order. From this you can identify the root letters for a particular verb, enabling you to look it up in Wehr's dictionary, and other similarly arranged references.

Part One:
Arabic Verbs

2 Regular verbs: The basic tenses

Arabic is relatively straightforward when it comes to tenses. Some languages have many tenses and are very specific about the time of an action and whether or not the action has been completed. Arabic grammar is vague about time and there are only two basic tenses:

• The *past* (or *perfect*) الماضِي

• The *present* (or *imperfect*) المَضارِع

The Past

In a simple regular verb, the basic past tense will look like this:

كَتَبَ (*kataba*): (he) wrote

شَرِبَ (*shariba*): (he) drank

حَمَلَ (*Hamala*): (he) carried

The three root letters are all followed by a vowel. In most cases this is all *fatHas (kataba/Hamala)*, but sometimes the second vowel is a *KaSra (shariba)*. (In rare cases, the second vowel is a *Damma (u)*, but you can ignore these verbs since you are not likely to see or use them.)

If we take off the final vowel, this هُوَ ("he"/"it") part of the verb (third person masculine singular) becomes the base, or *stem* of the past tense. Different endings can be added to this past stem depending on who is carrying out the action (the subject of the verb). So, كَتَبَ (*kataba*) is "he wrote" and كَتَب (*katab*) is the past stem. If we add the ending ت (*tu*) to the stem, it becomes كَتَبْتُ (*katabtu*) – "I wrote"; if we add نا (*naa*), it becomes كَتَبْنا (*katabnaa*) – "we wrote," etc. Here is a table showing all the endings for the past tense:

		Ending	Example

singular

أَنَا I	تُ (tu)	كَتَبْتُ (katabtu)
أَنْتَ you (masc.*)	تَ (ta)	كَتَبْتَ (katabta)
أَنْتِ you (fem.*)	تِ (ti)	كَتَبْتِ (katabti)
هُوَ he/it	ـَ (a)	كَتَبَ (kataba)
هِيَ she/it	تْ (at)	كَتَبَتْ (katabat)

plural

نَحْنُ we	نَا (naa)	كَتَبْنَا (katabnaa)
أَنْتُمْ you (masc. pl)	تُمْ (tum)	كَتَبْتُمْ (katabtum)
أَنتُنَّ you (fem. pl)	تُنَّ (tunna)	كَتَبْتُنَّ (katabtunna)
هُم they (masc.)	وا** (uu)	كَتَبُوا (katabuu)
هُنَّ they (fem.)	نَ (na)	كَتَبْنَ (katabna)

* For an explanation of masculine and feminine genders, see page 107.
** An extra *'alif* (ا) is written after the waaw (و) but is *silent.*

Note that you will not meet or need the feminine plurals as often as the masculine plurals. This is because you only use the feminine plural if all the people in a group are female. If the group is mixed male and female, the masculine is used. Therefore, this form is the most important to learn and become familiar with in the first place. There are also different endings for two people (the dual). To make it easier to absorb the basics first, an explanation of the dual and its associated verb endings has been separated. Refer to Chapters 17 and 28 for an explanation of the dual if you need it.

You do not have to use the personal pronouns (he, she, etc.) before the verb as you do in English. If you see an Arabic sentence like this:

كَتَبَت رِسالة لأُمِّهَا. (She) wrote a letter to her mother.

you can tell it is "she" because of the ending of the verb (*katabat*). The sentence could be more specific and say exactly <u>who</u> wrote the letter (the subject of the verb). Then you would see:

كَتَبَت فاطمة رِسالة لأُمِّهَا. Fatma wrote a letter to her mother.

Notice that in written Arabic the subject (Fatma) usually comes after the verb (wrote). More explanation of word order can be found in Chapter 11.

The Present

The present is used for an action (or state) which is still going on (unfinished). Whereas the past is formed by adding endings to a stem, the present adds letters on the beginning *and* end of a different present stem to show the subject of the verb. Look first at the present verb below. These letters on the beginning and end are underlined in the third column. Can you identify the stem that appears throughout?

singular

أَنا I	أَكْتُبُ	<u>'a</u>ktub(<u>u</u>*)
أَنتَ you (masc.)	تَكْتُبُ	<u>ta</u>ktub(<u>u</u>*)
أَنتِ you (fem.)	تَكْتُبِينَ	<u>ta</u>ktub<u>iina</u>
هُوَ he/it	يَكْتُبُ	<u>ya</u>ktub(<u>u</u>*)
هِيَ she/it	تَكْتُبُ	<u>ta</u>ktub(<u>u</u>*)

* The final ending *(u)* on some of the verbs above has been put in parentheses because it is not usually pronounced.

plural

نَحْنُ	we	نَكْتُبُ	naktub(u)
أَنْتُمْ	you (masc. pl)	تَكْتُبُونَ	taktubuuna
أَنْتُنَّ	you (fem. pl)	تَكْتُبْنَ	taktubna
هُم	they (masc.)	يَكْتُبُونَ	yaktubuuna
هُنَّ	they (fem.)	يَكْتُبْنَ	yaktubna

If you look at the table, you can see that the present stem — which appears in all the examples — is كْتُب *(ktub):* the three root letters *k/t/b*, with no vowel after the first letter and a *Damma* (ُ) after the second.

The different letters added on the beginning and end *(prefixes* and *suffixes)* are arranged around this present stem to show the subject of the verb. For example:

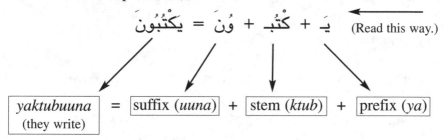

We can apply the same principle to another verb:

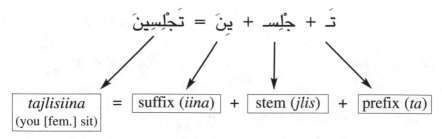

The present is used for both continuous and habitual actions or states, where in English we might use a different tense:

يَلْعَب الأَطْفال الكُرة يَوْم الجُمْعة.

The children <u>play</u> football on Friday(s).

يَجْلِس صَدِيقُكَ في مَقْعَدي!

Your friend <u>is sitting</u> in my chair!

As with the past, the vowel on the second root letter varies in the present. If the middle vowel on the past is a *kasra*, then it usually changes to a *fatHa* in the present:

shar<u>i</u>ba شَرِبَ (he drank)
yashr<u>a</u>b يَشْرَب (he drinks)

However, the majority of verbs have *fatHa* as the middle vowel of the past and, for these verbs, there is no rule to follow in the present. If you need to know the vowel, you can look in a dictionary where you will find the middle vowel written after the entry:

Remember that in most cases the middle vowel will not affect the meaning of the text or your understanding of it. Most Arabic is written without vowels and you will probably learn the more common middle vowels over time. Don't worry too much about this aspect. Native speakers will usually understand you as long as the root letters and the patterns are correct.

The Future

If you want to talk about the future in Arabic, you also use the present tense. Often the word سَوْفَ (*sawfa*) or the prefix سَـ (*sa*) are added to the front of the verb to indicate the future.

سَنَذْهَب إلى المَتْحَف المِصْريّ غَدًا.
We are going to the Egyptian museum tomorrow.

سَوْفَ يَزْرَع الفَلاَح البَطاطِس في الخَريف.
The farmer will plant potatoes in the Fall.

Summary of basic tenses

- There are only two basic tenses in Arabic:
  the past
  the present

- The past stem is formed from the three root letters with a *fatHa* after the first root and a *fatHa* (or sometimes a *kasra*) after the second root letter (*katab/sharib*). Endings are added to the stem to show the subject of the verb.

- The present stem is formed from the three root letters with a vowel after the second (*ktub/shrab/jlis*). Prefixes, and sometimes also endings, are added to the stem to show the subject of the verb.

- The future may be made by adding سَوْفَ (*sawfa*) or سَـ (*sa*) to the present.

---

3 Irregular verbs: introduction

Irregular verbs can be defined as verbs that act differently from the basic patterns in all or some cases. Unfortunately for the learner, Arabic has many irregular verbs (although some are more irregular than others!) These fall into three categories and include some of the most common verbs:

- Verbs with *waaw* (و) or *yaa'* (ي) as one of the root letters
- Verbs with *hamza* (ء) as one of the root letters
- *Doubled* verbs, where the second and third letters of the root are the same

The first category is the most common, and verbs in this category also display the most irregularities.

To help you remember the irregular verbs, we have chosen common verbs in each category to illustrate the patterns in which they appear. The verbs you see in the tables and examples in the following chapters are those you will probably encounter on a regular basis and will need to communicate in Arabic. By studying the way they work and meeting them frequently in spoken and written Arabic, these verbs should help to establish the irregular patterns in your mind.

The irregular verbs are covered first in the basic tenses (see Chapter 2 for a review of these tenses). Later chapters cover the various forms and variations. If you need to access this information immediately, go straight to the relevant chapter which will show you how each type of irregular verb behaves in these circumstances. If you want a general overview, work your way more systematically through the chapters in the order they are presented.

4 Irregular verbs: Verbs with *waaw* or *yaa'* as a root letter

Waaw (و) and *yaa'* (ي) are often called *weak letters*, and the verbs they contain called *weak verbs*. These letters do not have a strong sound, unlike letters such as *baa'* (ب) or *kaaf* (ك), and often drop out of words or become vowel sounds when put into the various patterns.

Weak verbs are the largest category of irregular verbs. They can be subdivided into three types depending on which of the root letters is affected:

- Verbs with *waaw* or *yaa'* as the <u>first</u> root letter (*assimilated* verbs)
- Verbs with *waaw* or *yaa'* as the <u>second</u> root letter (*hollow* verbs)
- Verbs with *waaw* or *yaa'* as the <u>third</u> root letter (*defective* verbs)

Waaw or yaa' as first root letter

This is one of the simplest irregular patterns.

- Verbs with *yaa'* as the first root letter are rare and almost completely regular.

- Verbs with *waaw* as the first root letter are regular in the past (perfect) tense:

وَجَدْنا عِلّة في البَرْنامَج.
We found a bug (flaw) in the program.

وَعَدَت الحُكومة بِتَخْفيض الضَّرائِب بَعْد الانْتِخابات.

The government promised a reduction in taxes after the elections.

وَصَلُوا إلى شيكاغو بالطائِرة.

They arrived in Chicago by airplane.

In the present, the first root letter almost always drops out completely:

يَصِل (*yaSil*) he arrives (from the root وصل)

يَجِدُون (*yajiduuna*) they find (from the root وجد)

تَضَع (*taDaع*) she puts (from the root وضع)   .

Compare this to the regular form of the present يَكْتُب (*yaktub*). In the assimilated verb, the first root letter has disappeared altogether from the stem, leaving just the second and third root letters (*Sil/jid/Daع*).

The table below shows more fully the present tense for the verb وَصَلَ/يَصِل (to arrive):

singular

أنا I	أَصِلُ	'aSil(u)
أَنْتَ you (masc.)	تَصِلُ	taSil(u)
أَنْتِ you (fem.)	تَصِلِينَ	taSiliina
هُوَ he/it	يَصِلُ	yaSil(u)
هِيَ she/it	تَصِلُ	taSil(u)

plural

نَحْنُ we	نَصِلُ	<u>naSil(u)</u>
أَنْتُمْ you (masc. pl)	تَصِلُونَ	<u>taSiluuna</u>
أَنْتُنَّ you (fem. pl)	تَصِلْنَ	<u>taSilna</u>
هُم they (masc.)	يَصِلُونَ	<u>yaSiluuna</u>
هُنَّ they (fem.)	يَصِلْنَ	<u>yaSilna</u>

Waaw or yaa' as second root letter

This group of verbs contains some of the most commonly used verbs in the Arabic language. They are called *hollow* verbs because the second (middle) root letter is often replaced by a long or short vowel.

Hollow verbs in the past

In the past tense, all hollow verbs have a long *aa* sound (ا) instead of the middle root letter for هو (he/it), هي (she/it) and هم (they):

كَانَ (*kaana* : "he/it was") from the root: كون
زَارَتْ (*zaarat* : "she visited") from the root: زور
بَاعُوا (*baaعuu* : "they sold") from the root: بيع
طَارَ (*Taara*: "he/it flew") from the root: طير

The other parts of the verb have a short vowel instead of the middle root letter (see separate chapter for dual verbs). This is usually a *Damma* if the middle root letter is a *waaw*, and a *kasra* if it is a *yaa'*:

كُنْتُ (*kuntu*: "I was") from the root: كون
زُرْنَا (*zurnaa*: "we visited") from the root: زور
بِعْتُمْ (*biعtum* : "you [pl.] sold") from the root: بيع
طِرْتِ (*Tirti*: "you [fem.] flew") from the root: طير

كانَ مَرِيضًا.

He was ill.

طارَت الطائِرة فَوْقَ الجِبال.

The airplane flew over the mountains.

هَلْ بِعتُم بَيْتكُمْ في نيو يورك؟

Have you sold your house in New York?

زُرْنَا المَتْحَف أمْس.

We visited the museum yesterday.

This table summarizes the past tense for hollow verbs:

singular	Verbs with *waaw** (زار to visit)	Verbs with *yaa'* (طار to fly)
أنا I	زُرْتُ (zurtu)	طِرْتُ (Tirtu)
أَنْتَ you (masc.)	زُرْتَ (zurta)	طِرْتَ (Tirta)
أَنْتِ you (fem.)	زُرْتِ (zurti)	طِرْتِ (Tirti)
هُوَ he/it	زَارَ (zaara)	طَارَ (Taara)
هِيَ she/it	زَارَتْ (zaarat)	طَارَتْ (Taarat)

plural		
نَحْنُ we	زُرْنَا (zurnaa)	طِرْنَا (Tirnaa)
أَنْتُمْ you (masc. pl)	زُرْتُمْ (zurtum)	طِرْتُمْ (Tirtum)
أَنتُنَّ you (fem. pl)	زُرْتُنَّ (zurtunna)	طِرْتُنَّ (Tirtunna)
هُم they (masc.)	زَارُوا (zaaruu)	طَارُوا (Taaruu)
هُنَّ they (fem.)	زُرْنَ (zurna)	طِرْنَ (Tirna)

* See page 24 for exceptions.

There are a few hollow verbs that behave in the past like verbs with *yaa'* as the middle root letter, but which actually have *waaw* in the middle. One of the most common verbs of this type is "to sleep," from the root letters نوم:

نامَتْ في سَرير أُمّها.

She slept in her mother's bed.

نِمْتُ حَتَّى الصَّبَاح.

I slept until morning.

From the table on page 23, you might have noticed that there is a short vowel in the middle of hollow verbs when there is a sukuun (ْ) over the <u>third</u> root letter. This is a general rule for hollow verbs and is worth remembering as it works for all types, tenses, and forms of hollow verbs:

> • **Sukuun** over third root letter of regular verb =
>   **short vowel** in the middle of irregular hollow verb
> • **Vowel** over third root letter of regular verb =
>   **long vowel** in the middle of irregular hollow verb

Hollow verbs in the present

In the present tense, hollow verbs also follow the rules highlighted above. Since the present tense usually has a vowel after the third root letter (even if this is not always pronounced), this means that hollow verbs in this tense are characterized mainly by a long vowel in the middle. The difference is that, whereas in the past the long vowel in the middle is always a long *aa* (*kaana*), in the present it is a long *ii* if the second root letter is a *yaa'* and usually a long *uu* if the second root letter is a *waaw*:

يَزُورُ (*yazuur[u]*: "he visits") from the root زور

يَبِيعُونَ (*yabiiʿuuna*: "they sell") from the root بيع

Verbs like نوم (see above) are the exception since they have a long *aa*

In the middle of the present:

يَنَامُ (*yanaam[u]*) he sleeps

يَنَامُونَ (*yanaamuuna*) they sleep

Here is a complete table and some examples showing the three different types of hollow verb in the present. Pay the most attention to learning the first two types. The third type has been included mainly for recognition. Notice that only the less common feminine plurals have a sukuun over the third root letter and a short vowel in the middle. As in the past, this vowel depends on the middle root letter.

	Most verbs with *waaw*		Verbs with *yaa'*		Verbs like نام، ينام	
singular						
أَنَا	أَزُورُ	(*'azuur[u]*)	أَطِيرُ	(*'aTiir[u]*)	أَنَامُ	(*'anaam[u]*)
أَنْتَ	تَزُورُ	(*tazuur[u]*)	تَطِيرُ	(*taTiir[u]*)	تَنَامُ	(*tanaam[u]*)
أَنْتِ	تَزُورِينَ	(*tazuuriina*)	تَطِيرِينَ	(*taTiiriina*)	تَنَامِينَ	(*tanaamiina*)
هُوَ	يَزُورُ	(*yazuur[u]*)	يَطِيرُ	(*yaTiir[u]*)	يَنَامُ	(*yanaam[u]*)
هِيَ	تَزُورُ	(*tazuur[u]*)	تَطِيرُ	(*taTiir[u]*)	تَنَامُ	(*tanaam[u]*)
plural						
نَحْنُ	نَزُورُ	(*nazuur[u]*)	نَطِيرُ	(*naTiir[u]*)	نَنَامُ	(*nanaam[u]*)
أَنْتُمْ	تَزُورُونَ	(*tazuuruuna*)	تَطِيرُونَ	(*taTiiruuna*)	تَنَامُونَ	(*tanaamuuna*)
أَنْتُنَّ	تَزُرْنَ	(*tazurna*)	تَطِرْنَ	(*taTirna*)	تَنَمْنَ	(*tanamna*)
هُم	يَزُورُونَ	(*yazuuruuna*)	يَطِيرُونَ	(*yaTiiruuna*)	يَنَامُونَ	(*yanaamuuna*)
هُنَّ	يَزُرْنَ	(*yazurna*)	يَطِرْنَ	(*yaTirna*)	يَنَمْنَ	(*yanamna*)

زَبوننا الرَئيسيّ يَزور مَكْتَبنا كُلّ شَهْر.

Our major client visits our office every month.

نَبيع المَحْصُول لتُجّار الجِمْلة.

We sell the crop to wholesalers.

أَنَام كُلّ يَوْم الساعة الثَانية عَشرة.

I go to sleep every day at twelve o'clock.

Waaw or yaa' as third root letter

This group of verbs is sometimes called *defective* verbs. There are three main types:

- Verbs with *waaw* as the last root letter.
- Verbs with *yaa'* as the last root letter and *fatHa* as the middle vowel in the past
- Verbs with *yaa'* as the last root letter and *kasra* as the middle vowel in the past

In the past tense, the first two types are reasonably regular. Only the parts of the verb for هو (he/it), هي (she/it) and هم (they) are irregular:

From the root شكو:

شَكَا (*shakaa*: "he complained")

شَكَتْ (*shakat*: "she complained")

شَكَوْا (*shakaw*: "they complained")

From the root مشي:

مَشَى (*mashaa*: "he walked")

مَشَتْ (*mashat*: "she walked")

مَشَوْا (*mashaw*: "they walked")

All of the irregular parts of these two types are pronounced the same. The only difference is the spelling of شكا (*shakaa*) with a final *'alif*, and مشى (*mashaa*) with a final *yaa'* (without the dots). (Look at Appendix (i) if you want to know more details about this final *yaa'* which is pronounced *aa* and known as *'alif maqsuura*.) The differences between these two types of verbs are more apparent in the regular parts of the past:

شَكَوْتُ (*shakawtu* : "I complained") from the root: شكو

مَشَيْنَا (*mashaynaa* : "we walked") from the root: مشي

رَمَيْتَ (*ramayta* : "you threw") from the root:رمي

رَجَوْتُمْ (*rajawtum*: "you [pl.] requested/hoped") from the root: رجو

Most defective verbs follow one of the two patterns above. However, there are some verbs with *yaa'* as the last root letter and *kasra* as the middle vowel that follow a different pattern. Two common examples are the verbs نَسِيَ (*nasiya* – to forget) and لَقِيَ (*laqiya* – to meet). These verbs have a long *ii* in many parts of the past tense, e.g. نَسِيتُ (*nasiitu*) – "I forgot."

The following table summarizes the past tense for all three main types of defective verbs:

	defective type 1 (شكا to complain)		defective type 2 (مشى to walk)		defective type 3 (نسي to forget)	
singular						
أنا	شَكَوْتُ	(shakawtu)	مَشَيْتُ	(mashaytu)	نَسِيتُ	(nasiitu)
أَنْتَ	شَكَوْتَ	(shakawta)	مَشَيْتَ	(mashayta)	نَسِيتَ	(nasiita)
أَنْتِ	شَكَوْتِ	(shakawti)	مَشَيْتِ	(mashayti)	نَسِيتِ	(nasiiti)
هُوَ	شَكَا	(shakaa)	مَشَى	(mashaa)	نَسِيَ	(nasiya)
هِيَ	شَكَتْ	(shakat)	مَشَتْ	(mashat)	نَسِيَتْ	(nasiyat)

	defective type 1 (شكا to complain)	defective type 2 (مشى to walk)	defective type 3 (نسي to forget)
plural			
نَحْنُ	شَكَوْنَا (shakawnaa)	مَشَيْنَا (mashaynaa)	نَسِينَا (nasiinaa)
أَنْتُمْ	شَكَوْتُمْ (shakawtum)	مَشَيْتُمْ (mashaytum)	نَسِيتُمْ (nasiitum)
أَنْتُنَّ	شَكَوْتُنَّ (shakawtunna)	مَشَيْتُنَّ (mashaytunna)	نَسِيتُنَّ (nasiitunna)
هُمْ	شَكَوْا (shakaw)	مَشَوْا (mashaw)	نَسُوا (nasuu)
هُنَّ	شَكَوْنَ (shakawna)	مَشَيْنَ (mashayna)	نَسِينَ (nasiina)

Here are the three types of defective verbs in the present tense:

	defective type 1 (يشكو to complain)	defective type 2 (يمشي to walk)	defective type 3 (ينسى to forget)
singular			
أنَا	أَشْكُو ('ashkuu)	أَمْشِي ('amshii)	أَنْسَى ('ansaa)
أَنْتَ	تَشْكُو (tashkuu)	تَمْشِي (tamshii)	تَنْسَى (tansaa)
أَنْتِ	تَشْكِينَ (tashkiina*)	تَمْشِينَ (tamshiina*)	تَنْسَيْنَ (tansayna)
هُوَ	يَشْكُو (yashkuu)	يمْشِي (yamshii)	يَنْسَى (yansaa)
هِيَ	تَشْكُو (tashkuu)	تَمْشِي (tamshii)	تَنْسَى (tansaa)
plural			
نَحْنُ	نَشْكُو (nashkuu)	نمْشِي (namshii)	نَنْسَى (nansaa)
أَنْتُمْ	تَشْكُونَ (tashkuuna*)	تَمْشُونَ (tamshuuna*)	تَنْسَوْنَ (tansawna)
أَنْتُنَّ	تَشْكُونَ (tashkuuna)	تَمْشِينَ (tamshiina)	تَنْسَيْنَ (tansayna)
هُمْ	يَشْكُونَ (yashkuuna*)	يَمْشُونَ (yamshuuna*)	يَنْسَوْنَ (yansawna)
هُنَّ	يَشْكُونَ (yashkuuna)	يمْشِينَ (yamshiina)	يَنْسَيْنَ (yansayna)

Notice that the weak third root letter drops out altogether in these cases.

Notice that defective verbs in the present tense can usually be spotted because they have a long vowel instead of the third root letter. In type 1 this is a long *uu* (*yashkuu*); in type 2 a long *ii* (*yamshii*) and in type 3 a long *aa* (*yansaa*) — but note this is written with *'alif maqsura*, see Appendix (i). Some of the changes that happen are not very logical and can be difficult to remember. Concentrate on the most common parts first. Leave the other parts (e.g., feminine plural) until you feel confident with the basic patterns.

Summary of weak verbs

- Weak verbs are those which have *waaw* (و) or *yaa'* (ي) as one of the root letters.

- There are three types of weak verb:
  Verbs with *waaw* or *yaa'* as the <u>first</u> root letter (*assimilated* verbs)
  Verbs with *waaw* or *yaa'* as the <u>second</u> root letter (*hollow* verbs)
  Verbs with *waaw* or *yaa'* as the <u>third</u> root letter (*defective* verbs)

- *Assimilated* verbs are mainly regular except the first root letter almost always drops out in the present tense.

- *Hollow* verbs have a vowel in the middle instead of the second root letter. This is a *short* vowel if the <u>third</u> root letter has a sukuun (ْ) over it, and a *long* vowel if it does not.

- *Defective* verbs are characterized by a long vowel (*aa/uu/ii*) or a diphthong (*ay/aw*) instead of the third root letter, but do not always behave predictably. Each pattern should be learned individually.

5 Irregular verbs: Doubled verbs

Doubled verbs are those where the third root letter is the same as the second root letter. They are one of the simplest forms of irregular verbs to master. The general rule is similar to the rule for hollow verbs and is dependent on the vowel over the <u>third</u> root letter:

> • **Sukuun** over third root letter of regular verb =
> second and third root letters **written separately** in doubled verb
> • **Vowel** over third root letter of regular verb =
> second and third root letters **written together** in doubled verb

For example, the past tense pattern كَتَبُوا (*katabuu* – they wrote) has the vowel *Damma* (ـُ) over the third root letter. So, in a doubled verb, the second and third root letters would be written together with a *shadda* (ـّ) in this pattern:

شَكُّوا (*shakkuu* : "they doubted") from the root: شَكَ

رَدَّتْ (*raddat* : "she replied") from the root: رَدّ

However, the past tense pattern كَتَبْنَا (*katabnaa* – "we wrote") has a *sukuun* (ـْ) over the third root letter. So in a doubled verb, the second and third root letters would be written separately in this pattern:

شَكَكْنَا (*shakaknaa* : "we doubted")

رَدَدْتُ (*radadtu* : "I replied")

The same rules apply to the present tense (look back at Chapter 2 if you need to remind yourself of the patterns for regular verbs).

As most parts of the present tense have a vowel after the third root letter, this means that you will see the root letters in a doubled verb written together in most cases. In addition, the middle vowel of the present tense (mostly *Damma* in doubled verbs) shifts back over the first root letter:

أَوَدّ أَنْ أَشْكُرَكَ عَلَى خِطابِكَ الأخير.

I'd like to thank you for your last letter.

سَأَمُدُّكَ بِالمَعْلومات الّتي طَلَبْتَها فَوْرًا.

I will send you the information you requested immediately.

Here is a table summarizing the past and present patterns for doubled verbs. A good exercise is to cover the column showing the doubled verb and see if you can predict the pattern according to the rules on page 30.

singular	Doubled verbs in the past	Doubled verbs in the present
أنا I	رَدَدْتُ radadtu	أَرُدُّ 'arudd(u)
أَنْتَ you (masc.)	رَدَدْتَ radadta	تَرُدُّ tarudd(u)
أَنْتِ you (fem.)	رَدَدْتِ radadti	تَرُدِّينَ taruddiina
هُوَ he/it	رَدَّ radda	يَرُدُّ yarudd(u)
هِيَ she/it	رَدَّتْ raddat	تَرُدُّ tarudd(u)

plural		
نَحْنُ we	رَدَدْنَا radadnaa	نَرُدُّ narudd(u)
أَنْتُمْ you (masc. pl)	رَدَدْتُمْ radadtum	تَرُدُّونَ tarudduuna
أَنْتُنَّ you (fem. pl)	رَدَدْتُنَّ radadtunna	تَرْدُدْنَ tardudna
هُم they (masc.)	رَدُّوا radduu	يَرُدُّونَ yarudduuna
هُنَّ they (fem.)	رَدَدْنَ radadna	يَرْدُدْنَ yardudna

A final cautionary note about doubled verbs: many spoken dialects treat these verbs in the past like verbs with *yaa'* as the final root letter (see Defective verbs, Chapter 4). This means that many native speakers would say رَدَيْنا (*radaynaa*) for "we replied" rather than the grammatically correct رَدَدْنا (*radadnaa*). In fact, this is also a common written error among native speakers. This can be confusing to a learner and is worth a special mention.

Summary of doubled verbs

- Doubled verbs have the same second and third root letter.

- There are simple rules governing the way these verbs behave: the doubled root letters are written separately if the <u>third</u> root letter has a sukuun (̊) over it, and written together if it does not.

6 Irregular verbs: Verbs with *hamza*

The *hamza* can be an enigmatic letter. The nearest analogy in English is the apostrophe. In both cases there is uncertainty as to when and how to use it, even among native speakers. The apostrophe causes more errors in English than virtually anything else and the *hamza* probably has this dubious distinction in Arabic. Whereas in English we ask ourselves: "Should the apostrophe come before the *s* or after the *s*?," in Arabic the question becomes: "Which letter should carry the *hamza*?" When you review this chapter, it is always worth reminding yourself that you are not alone in finding the *hamza* sometimes elusive. Read the general guidelines but be prepared to refer to the tables regularly.

The *hamza* itself is considered a consonant, not a vowel, pronounced as a short glottal stop — see Appendix (i) for more detail on pronunciation. Many verbs have *hamza* as one of the root letters. It can be any of the three root letters and is found in some common verbs.

Like the apostrophe, the rules (such as they exist) for *hamza* are more concerned with where to place it than how to pronounce it. Verbs with *hamza* as one of the root letters are mainly regular. The changes that occur are in the letter that carries the *hamza*.

There are some guidelines for writing *hamza*. The simplest way to predict how a particular pattern will be written is to look at the pattern for regular verbs (see Chapter 2), and then apply the general rules on the following page. Remember that there are exceptions and alternatives. For individual verbs, check the tables in this chapter and in the relevant chapters for derived forms or other patterns.

General rules for verbs with *hamza* as one of the root letters

- If the *hamza* is at the beginning of the verb, it is written on an *'alif*: أَخَذَ (he took)/ أَكَلُوا (they ate)

- If a pattern means you would need to write two *'alifs,* then these are combined as one with a madda sign over it (آ), pronounced as a long *aa*: آخُذ – *'aakhudh* (I take), instead of أَأْخُذ

- Otherwise, the letter carrying the *hamza* tends to relate to the vowel <u>before</u> the *hamza*:
  - *Damma* before *hamza* = *hamza* written on *waaw* (ؤ)
  - *Kasra* before *hamza* = *hamza* written on *yaa'* without dots (ئ or ـئـ)
  - *FatHa* before *hamza* = *hamza* written on *'alif* (أ)

- If the *hamza* has no vowel before it (i.e., the letter before has a *sukuun* over it), then the rules above default to the vowel over the *hamza* itself: يَسْأَل (he asks)

Examples:

قَرَأْنَا مَسْرَحِيّة عَرَبِيّة في الفَصْل.
We read an Arabic play in class.

سَأَلْتُ المُدَرِّس سُؤالاً عَن المُؤَلِّف .
I asked the teacher a question about the author.

قَالَ إنّ المُؤَلِّف كَتَبَ المسرحيّة في السَبْعِينات...
He said that the author wrote the play in the seventies...

...لأَنَّه سَئِمَ من عَمَلِهِ في البَنْك.
...because he was fed up with his work in the bank.

Don't worry if these rules seem complicated. In the basic tenses there are very few other irregularities, and the majority of patterns are written with the *hamza* on an *'alif*. If you refer to the tables on page

35, you will start to get a feel for how to write these verbs.
Look at the general rules on page 34 in conjunction with the later
chapters if you need to find out how the verbs with *hamza* behave in
the derived forms or other patterns.

Past tense

	Hamza as root 1 (أَخَذ: to take)	**Hamza as root 2** (سأل: to ask)	**Hamza as root 3** (بطُئ: to be slow*)
singular			
أَنا	أَخَذْتُ ('akhadhtu)	سَأَلْتُ (sa'altu)	بَطُؤْتُ (baTu'tu)
أَنْتَ	أَخَذْتَ ('akhadhta)	سَأَلْتَ (sa'alta)	بَطُؤْتَ (baTu'ta)
أَنْتِ	أَخَذْتِ ('akhadhti)	سَأَلْتِ (sa'alti)	بَطُؤْتِ (baTu'ti)
هُوَ	أَخَذَ ('akhadha)	سَأَلَ (sa'ala)	بَطُؤَ (baTu'a)
هِيَ	أَخَذَتْ ('akhadhat)	سَأَلَتْ (sa'alat)	بَطُؤَتْ (baTu'at)
plural			
نَحْنُ	أَخَذْنَا ('akhadhnaa)	سَأَلْنَا (sa'alnaa)	بَطُؤْنَا (baTu'naa)
أَنْتُمْ	أَخَذْتُمْ ('akhadhtum)	سَأَلْتُمْ (sa'altum)	بَطُؤْتُمْ (baTu'tum)
أَنْتُنَّ	أَخَذْتُنَّ ('akhadhtunna)	سَأَلْتُنَّ (sa'altunna)	بَطُؤْتُنَّ (baTu'tunna)
هُمْ	أَخَذُوا ('akhadhuu)	سَأَلُوا (sa'aluu)	بَطُؤُوا (baTu'uu)
هُنَّ	أَخَذْنَ ('akhadhna)	سَأَلْنَ (sa'alna)	بَطُؤْنَ (baTu'na)

*This verb is one of a very few that have *Damma* as the vowel on the middle root
letter (i.e., the ط)in the past. It has been chosen to show how the *hamza* is usually
written when preceded by a *Damma*.

Present tense

	Hamza as root 1 (يَأخَذ: to take)		Hamza as root 2 (يسأل: to ask)		Hamza as root 3 (يبطؤ: to be slow)	
singular						
أنا	آخَذ ('aakhudh[u])	أسأَل	('as'al[u])	أبْطؤ	('abTu'[u])	
أَنْتَ	تَأخَذ (ta'khudh[u])	تَسأَل	(tas'al[u])	تَبْطؤ	(tabTu'[u])	
أَنْتِ	تَأخَذِينَ (ta'khudhiina)	تَسأَلِينَ	(tas'aliina)	تَبْطُؤِينَ	(tabTu'iina)	
هُوَ	يَأخَذ (ya'khudh[u])	يَسأَل	(yas'al[u])	يَبْطؤ	(yabTu'[u])	
هِيَ	تَأخَذ (ta'khudh[u])	تَسأَل	(tas'al[u])	تَبْطُؤ	(tabTu'[u])	

plural						
نَحْنُ	نَأخَذ (na'khudh[u])	نَسأَل	(nas'al[u])	نَبْطؤ	(nabTu'[u])	
أَنْتُمْ	تَأخَذُونَ (ta'khudhuuna)	تَسأَلُونَ	(tas'aluuna)	تَبْطُؤُونَ	(tabTu'uuna)	
أَنْتُنَّ	تَأخَذْنَ (ta'khudhna)	تَسأَلْنَ	(tas'alna)	تَبْطُؤْنَ	(tabTu'na)	
هُم	يَأخَذُونَ (ya'khudhuuna)	يَسأَلُونَ	(yas'aluuna)	يَبْطُؤُونَ	(yabTu'uuna)	
هُنَّ	يَأخَذْنَ (ya'khudhna)	يَسأَلْنَ	(yas'alna)	يَبْطُؤْنَ	(yabTu'na)	

Remember that in the present tense the middle vowel will vary, as it does with regular verbs (see page 17). In the case of verbs with *hamza* as the second or third root letter, this could affect the spelling, although a middle *fatHa* with the *hamza* carried by an *'alif* (أ) is by far the most common.

Summary of verbs with *hamza*

- Irregularities in these verbs are mainly concerned with the spelling (which letter carries the *hamza*).

- There are some general rules which help to determine how the *hamza* should be written.

- There are also exceptions and alternatives which need to be individually absorbed over time.

7 Derived forms of verbs: Introduction

While Arabic is not rich in tenses, it makes up for this with its system of verb patterns, or *forms*. All the verbs covered in Chapters 1 to 6 have been the basic, or *root*, form of the verb. The Arabic language plays with this root to add subtle variations to the meaning.

If you look at these groups of words in English, you can see they have different but connected meanings:

liquidate
liquefy
liquidize

validate
value
revalue

By adding different endings and prefixes, the meaning is slightly changed. For example, as a native speaker you recognize that the prefix "re-" means "to do something again."

Arabic takes this principle much further with many different patterns that add meaning to the original root form. These *derived* forms are the major way in which Arabic achieves its richness of vocabulary. Look at the following examples, all derived from the same root

قَتَلُوا (*qataluu*) they killed

قَتَّلُوا (*qattaluu*) they massacred ("killed intensely")

قَاتَلُوا (*qaataluu*) they battled ("tried to kill")

تَقَاتَلُوا (*taqaataluu*) they fought each other

All these are different forms of the same root قتل (*q/t/l*). The verb ending associated with "they" in the past (*uu*) stays the same, but different letters have been added between and before the root to add to the original meaning.

There are eight significant derived forms. Some others exist, but are only seen in poetry or archaic texts. Western scholars of Arabic refer to the forms by Latin numbers: form II ("form two"), form III, form IV, etc. However, native speakers will not be familiar with this. They will know them by the <u>present tense</u> of the pattern, using the root فعل (f/ع/l) — see Chapter 1 for more about this. For example, the verb قاتلوا (they battled), shown in the examples earlier, would be referred to as form III by Arabists, but as the pattern يفاعِل (*yufaaع il*) by native speakers and Arab grammarians. In the following chapters, we will refer to the forms by their numbers, with the فعل pattern in brackets.

Most of the forms are connected with certain meanings — such as trying to do something, doing something together, etc. — although sometimes these meanings have strayed over time or have been adopted for a new concept. All the derived forms do not exist for all roots, but most roots have at least one or two forms in general circulation. You will need to look in a dictionary under the root to know exactly which forms exist. In addition, Arabic speakers will sometimes make up new verbs from existing roots, either as a joke or in an effort to be creative or poetic.

Although the derived forms can at first seem complicated, they are in fact a useful aid for the learner. If you recognize a derived pattern and know another word with the same root, you can often take a good guess at the meaning even if you have never seen that particular word before. The next three chapters will show you the derived patterns and meanings connected with them, as well as any differences in how the irregular verbs behave in these forms.

8 Derived forms II–IV

The first of the three main groups of derived forms is made up of forms II (يُفَعِّل – yufaعع il), III (يُفاعِل – yufaaع il), and IV (يُفْعِل – yufع il).

Characteristics

Past tense
• Form II is made by doubling the second root letter of the basic verb:

فَعَلَ (basic verb faع ala) ➜ فَعَّلَ (form II verb faعع ala)

• Form III is made by adding a long *aa* (ا) after the second root letter:

فَعَلَ (basic verb faع ala) ➜ فَاعَلَ (form III verb faaع ala)

• Form IV is formed by adding an *'alif* before the first root letter and a *sukuun* (ـْ) over it:

فَعَلَ (basic verb faع ala) ➜ أَفْعَلَ (form IV verb 'afع ala)

Present tense
In the present tense, these three forms have a *Damma* (ـُ) as the first vowel and a *kasra* (ـِ) as the last. Forms II and III have a *fatHa* (ـَ) over the first root letter. Form IV has a *sukuun* over the first root letter, as in the past tense:

Form II: يُفَعِّل (*yufaعع il*)
Form III: يُفَاعِل (*yufaaع il*)
Form IV: يُفْعِل (*yufع il*)

It is worth noting that forms II, III and IV are the only verb forms that have a *Damma* as the opening vowel.

Common meaning patterns

1. Forms II and IV can have the meaning of carrying out an action to someone/something else (making a verb *transitive* or *causative*):

يَدْرُس (basic verb *yadrus* – to study)→
يُدَرِّس (form II verb *yudarris* – to teach)

يَسْخُن (basic verb *yaskhun* – to become hot)→
يُسَخِّن (form II verb *yusakhkhin* – to heat ["to make something hot"])

يَخْرُج (basic verb *yakhruj* – to go out)→
يُخْرِج (form IV verb *yukhrij* – to remove/eject ["to take something out"])

Sometimes a root can be put into forms II <u>and</u> IV with the same, or almost the same, meaning. Watch for the subtle differences, e.g.:

يَعْلَم (basic verb *yaɛlam* – to know)→
يُعَلِّم (form II verb *yuɛallim* – to instruct), and…
يُعْلِم (form IV verb *yuɛlim* – to inform)

2. Form II can also give a verb the meaning of doing something intensively and/or repeatedly:

يَقْتُل (basic verb *yaqtul* – to kill)→
يُقَتِّل (form II verb *yuqattil* – to massacre)

يَكْسَر (basic verb *yaksar* – to break)→
يُكَسِّر (form II verb *yukassir* – to smash up)

3. Form III often carries the meaning of "doing something with someone else":

يَجْلِس (basic verb *yajlis* – to sit)→
يُجالِس (form III verb *yujaalis* – to sit with [someone])

يَعْمَل (basic verb *yaɛmal* – to do)→
يُعامِل (form III verb *yuɛaamil* – to treat/deal with [someone])

4. Form III can also carry the meaning of "trying to do something":

يَقْتُل (basic verb *yaqtul* – to kill)➔

يُقَاتِل (form II verb *yuqaatil* – to battle ["to try to kill"])

يَسْبِق (basic verb *yasbiq* – to come before/precede)➔

يُسَابِق (form III verb *yusaabiq* – to race ["to try to come before"])

The verb "to try" is itself a form III verb:

يُحاوِل (*yuHaawil*)

Here is a table showing the past and present tenses for these three verb forms, followed by some example sentences:

Past

	Form II (faɛɛala)		Form III (faaɛala)		Form IV ('afɛala)	
singular						
أنا	دَرَّسْتُ	(darrastu)	سابَقْتُ	(saabaqtu)	أعْلَمْتُ	('aɛlamtu)
أَنْتَ	دَرَّسْتَ	(darrasta)	سابَقْتَ	(saabaqta)	أعْلَمْتَ	('aɛlamta)
أَنْتِ	دَرَّسْتِ	(darrasti)	سابَقْتِ	(saabaqti)	أعْلَمْتِ	('aɛlamti)
هُوَ	دَرَّسَ	(darrasa)	سابَقَ	(saabaqa)	أعْلَمَ	('aɛlama)
هِيَ	دَرَّسَتْ	(darrasat)	سابَقَتْ	(saabaqat)	أعْلَمَتْ	('aɛlamat)

plural						
نَحْنُ	دَرَّسْنا	(darrasnaa)	سابَقْنا	(saabaqnaa)	أعْلَمْنا	('aɛlamnaa)
أَنْتُمْ	دَرَّسْتُمْ	(darrastum)	سابَقْتُمْ	(saabaqtum)	أعْلَمْتُمْ	('aɛlamtum)
أَنْتُنَّ	دَرَّسْتُنَّ	(darrastunna)	سابَقْتُنَّ	(saabaqtunna)	أعْلَمْتُنَّ	('aɛlamtunna)
هُم	دَرَّسوا	(darrasuu)	سابَقوا	(saabaquu)	أعْلَمُوا	('aɛlamuu)
هُنَّ	دَرَّسْنَ	(darrasna)	سابَقْنَ	(saabaqna)	أعْلَمْنَ	('aɛlamna)

Present

	Form II (yufaʕʕil)	Form III (yufaaʕil)	Form IV (yufʕil)
singular			
أنا	أُدَرِّس ('udarris[u])	أُسابِق ('usaabiq[u])	أُعْلِم ('uʕlim[u])
أنْتَ	تُدَرِّس (tudarris[u])	تُسابِق (tusaabiq[u])	تُعْلِم (tuʕlim[u])
أنْتِ	تُدَرِّسينَ (tudarrisiina)	تُسابِقينَ (tusaabiqiina)	تُعْلِمينَ (tuʕlimiina)
هُوَ	يُدَرِّس (yudarris[u])	يُسابِق (yusaabiq[u])	يُعْلِم (yuʕlim[u])
هِيَ	تُدَرِّس (tudarris[u])	تُسابِق (tusaabiq[u])	تُعْلِم (tuʕlim[u])

	Form II	Form III	Form IV
plural			
نَحْنُ	نُدَرِّس (nudarris[u])	نُسابِق (nusaabiq[u])	نُعْلِم (nuʕlim[u])
أنْتُمْ	تُدَرِّسونَ (tudarrisuuna)	تُسابِقونَ (tusaabiquuna)	تُعْلِمونَ (tuʕlimuuna)
أنْتُنَّ	تُدَرِّسْنَ (tudarrisna)	تُسابِقْنَ (tusaabiqna)	تُعْلِمْنَ (tuʕlimna)
هُم	يُدَرِّسونَ (yudarrisuuna)	يُسابِقونَ (yusaabiquuna)	يُعْلِمونَ (yuʕlimuuna)
هُنَّ	يُدَرِّسْنَ (yudarrisna)	يُسابِقْنَ (yusaabiqna)	يُعْلِمْنَ (yuʕlimna)

صَيْد السَمَك يُعَلِّم الصَبْر.

Fishing [*lit*: hunting fish] teaches patience.

سَنُحاوِل اليَوْم أَن نَذْهَب إلَى النَّهر.

We will try to go to the river today.

الشَمْس القَوِّية سَخَّنَت الماء.

The hot [*lit:* strong] sun has warmed the water.

العُمّال أخْرَجوا الزَبالة.

The workers have removed the garbage.

حَمَّلْنا المِلَفّ مِن الإنترنَت أمْس.

We downloaded the file from the Internet yesterday.

Irregular verbs in forms II–IV

Verbs that are irregular in the basic form often also show irregularities in the derived forms. You should still try to apply the same basic rules for the different types of irregular verb: weak verbs, doubled verbs, and verbs with *hamza* as a root letter (see Chapters 4–6). Note that, in general, if a form requires doubling a root letter or separating root letters with a long vowel, then a basic verb with a doubled or weak root letter (*waaw* or *yaa'*) will often behave perfectly regularly when put into these patterns. Here are some notes about how irregular verbs behave in forms II–IV, followed by a summary table:

Doubled verbs:
• Doubled verbs behave as *regular* verbs in form II. (Doubling the middle root letter means that the second and third root letters of a doubled verb are always written separately.)
• Doubled verbs in forms III and IV follow the same rules as for the basic doubled verb (see page 30). Form IV doubled verbs are much more common than form III.

Verbs with *hamza* as a root letter:
• Verbs with *hamza* behave roughly as *regular* verbs, but see rules about spelling on page 30. Note in particular the rule about writing two *hamzas* carried by *'alif* together as a *madda* (آ). This rule means the past tense of forms III and IV starts with this combination when *hamza* is the first root letter (see table).
• When *hamza* is the middle (second) root letter, you may see it by itself on the line in form III because it follows a long vowel (see page 34).

Weak verbs:
• Verbs with *waaw* or *yaa'* as the first or second root letter (*assimilated* and *hollow* verbs) behave as *regular* verbs in forms II and III.
• *Assimilated* verbs in form IV have a long *uu* vowel at the beginning of the present tense (see table).
• *Hollow* verbs in form IV behave as they do in the basic pattern. They have a short vowel in the middle if the third root letter has a *sukuun* over it, but this is the short vowel connected to the <u>derived</u> pattern

and not to the original root. For example, "I wanted" = أَرَدْتُ ('aradtu). The short vowel is a *fatHa* because the form IV past pattern is أَفْعَلَ ('afala).

- Verbs with *waaw* or *yaa'* as the third root (*defective*) behave irregularly in all forms. Forms II, III and IV *defective* verbs all have the same endings as the يمشي/مشى basic group of verbs (see pages 27–28).

	Form II (*yufaععil*)		**Form III** (*yufaaعil*)		**Form IV** (*yufعil*)	
oubled verbs						
past	رَدَّدَ	repeated	ضادَّ	opposed	أَحَبَّ	liked
present	يُرَدِّد	repeats	يُضادَّ	opposes	يُحِبَّ	likes
erbs with hamza						
1st root letter:						
past	أَثَّرَ	influenced	آخَذَ	blamed	آمَنَ	believed (in)
present	يُؤَثِّر	influences	يُوَاخِذ	blames	يُؤْمِن	believes (in)
2nd root letter:						
past	*no verbs in*		سَاءَلَ	questioned	أَسْأَمَ	bored
present	*common circulation*		يُسَائِل	questions	يُسْئِم	bores
3nd root letter:						
past	هَنَّأَ	congratulated	كافَأَ	rewarded	أَنْشَأَ	founded
present	يُهَنِّئ	congratulates	يكافِئ	rewards	يُنْشِئ	founds
Weak verbs						
ssimilated:						
past	يَسَّرَ \ وَصَّلَ	facilitated/ delivered	وافَقَ	agreed with	أَوْصَلَ	connected
present	يُيَسِّر \ يُوَصِّل	facilitates/ delivers	يُوَافِق	agrees with	يُوصِل	connects
ollow:						
past	خَوَّفَ	frightened	نَاوَلَ	handed over	أَرَادَ	wanted
present	يُخَوِّف	frightens	يُنَاوِل	hands over	يُرِيد	wants
efective:						
past	رَبَّى	bred/raised	لاقَى	met with	أَعْطَى	gave
present	يُرَبِّي	breeds/raises	يُلاقِي	meets with	يُعْطِي	gives

Summary of forms II–IV

- Form II verbs are characterized by the doubling of the second root letter (يُفَعِّل – *yufaععil*).

- Form III verbs are characterized by the long *aa* vowel after the first root letter (يُفَاعِل – *yufaaعil*).

- Form IV verbs are characterized by the *sukuun* over the first root letter (يُفْعِل – *yufعil*).

- Forms II–IV are the only Arabic verbs to have a *Damma* as the first vowel in the present tense (*yudarris, nuHaawil*, etc.)

- Forms II and IV are most often used with a *transitive* or *causative* meaning (doing something <u>to</u> something/someone else). Form III is most often used for mutual actions (doing something <u>with</u> someone else). However, there are also many other possible meaning patterns.

- Verbs that are irregular in the basic form may also act irregularly in the derived forms (see table on page 41).

9 Derived forms V–VI

The second of the groups of derived forms is made up of
forms V (يَتَفَعَّل – *yatafaʿʿal*) and VI (يَتَفَاعَل – *yatafaaʿal*).

Characteristics

Past tense
- Form V is made by adding تَ (*ta*) on the front of the form II pattern:

  فَعَّل (form II *faʿʿala*) → تَفَعَّل (form V verb *tafaʿʿala*)

- Form VI is made by adding تَ (*ta*) on the front of the form III pattern:

  فَاعَل (form III *faaʿala*) → تَفَاعَل (form VI verb *tafaaʿala*)

Present tense
In the present tense, these two forms are vowelized throughout with
fatHa (ـَ):

  Form V: يَتَفَعَّل (*yatafaʿʿal*)
  Form VI: يَتَفَاعَل (*yatafaaʿal*)

Common meaning patterns

1. Form V can be connected to form II in meaning as well as structure.
Form V is often the *reflexive* of form II. In other words, it has the
meaning of performing an action <u>on yourself</u>:

يُذَكِّر (form II verb *yudhakkir* – to remind)→
يَتَذَكَّر (form V verb *yatadhakkar* – to remember ["remind yourself"])

Notice that this can mean some form V verbs are very close in meaning to the original basic root verb and can even sometimes be alternatives with almost the same meaning:

يَعْلَم (basic verb *yaε lam* – to know)→

يُعَلِّم (form II verb *yuε allim* – to instruct)→

يَتَعَلَّم (form V verb *yataε allam* – to learn)

2. As form V is often the reflexive of form II, so form VI is sometimes the reflexive of form III, producing the meaning of doing something together or as a group:

يُعاوِن (form III verb *yuε aawin* – to help)→

يَتَعَاوَن (form IV verb *yataε aawan* – to cooperate ["to help each other"])

يُحادِث (form III verb *yuHaadith* – to talk to someone)→

يَتَحادَث (form VI verb *yataHaadath* – to converse/talk together

3. Some form VI verbs are connected with a state, where in English we might use an adjective ("to be lazy," "to be annoyed," etc.). You should also be aware that there are also many form V and VI verbs that have no particular logic (or the logic is lost in the history of the language):

يَتَكاسَل (*yatakaasal*) – to be lazy

يَتَضايَق (*yataDaayaq*) – to be annoyed

يَتَوَقَّف (*yatawaqqaf*)– to stop

يَتَصَرَّف (*yataSarraf*) – to behave

Here is a table showing the past and present tenses of forms V and VI, followed by some example sentences:

Past

singular	**Form V** *(tafaɛɛala)*		**Form VI** *(tafaaɛala)*	
أنا	تَذَكَّرْتُ	(tadhakkartu)	تَحَادَثْتُ	(taHaadathtu)
أَنْتَ	تَذَكَّرْتَ	(tadhakkarta)	تَحَادَثْتَ	(taHaadathta)
أَنْتِ	تَذَكَّرْتِ	(tadhakkarti)	تَحَادَثْتِ	(taHaadathti)
هُوَ	تَذَكَّرَ	(tadhakkara)	تَحَادَثَ	(taHaadatha)
هِيَ	تَذَكَّرَتْ	(tadhakkarat)	تَحَادَثَتْ	(taHaadathat)

plural

نَحْنُ	تَذَكَّرْنا	(tadhakkarnaa)	تَحَادَثْنا	(taHaadathnaa)
أَنْتُمْ	تَذَكَّرْتُمْ	(tadhakkartum)	تَحَادَثْتُمْ	(taHaadathtum)
أَنْتُنَّ	تَذَكَّرْتُنَّ	(tadhakkartunna)	تَحَادَثْتُنَّ	(taHaadathtunna)
هُم	تَذَكَّروا	(tadhakkaruu)	تَحَادَثوا	(taHaadathuu)
هُنَّ	تَذَكَّرْنَ	(tadhakkarna)	تَحَادَثْنَ	(taHaadathna)

Present

	Form V *(yatafaεεal)*	Form VI *(yatafaaεal)*
singular		
أنا	أَتَذَكَّر ('atadhakkar[u])	أَتَحادَث ('ataHaadath[u])
أَنْتَ	تَتَذَكَّر (tatadhakkar[u])	تَتَحَّادَث (tataHaadath[u])
أَنْتِ	تَتَذَكَّرِينَ (tatadhakkariina)	تَتَحادَثينَ (tataHaadathiina)
هُوَ	يَتَذَكَّر (yatadhakkar[u])	يَتَحادَث (yataHaadath[u])
هِيَ	تَتَذَكَّر (tatadhakkar[u])	تَتَحادَث (tataHaadath[u])

plural		
نَحْنُ	نَتَذَكَّر (natadhakkar[u])	نَتَحادَث (nataHaadath[u])
أَنْتُمْ	تَتَذَكَّرونَ (tatadhakkaruuna)	تَتَحادَثون (tataHaadathuuna)
أَنتُن	تَتَذَكَّرْنَ (tatadhakkarna)	تَتَحادَثْنَ (tataHaadathna)
هُم	يَتَذَكَّرونَ (yatadhakkaruuna)	يَتَحادَثونَ (yataHaadathuuna)
هُنَّ	يَتَذَكَّرْنَ (yatadhakkarna)	يَتَحادَثْنَ (yataHaadathna)

أَنا لا أَتَذَكَّر اسمَكَ.

I don't remember your name.

تَكاسَلْتُ في الصَّباح فَفاتَني القِطار.

I was lazy in the morning, and so I missed the train.

بَعْض الناس يَتَصَرَّفون بِطَريقة غَريبة.

Some people behave in a strange manner.

تَلَوَّثَ الشاطِئ بَعدَ حادِث السَفينة.

The coast was polluted after the ship's accident.

هَلْ تَتَضايَق مِن الدُّخان؟

Does the smoke bother you?

Irregular verbs in forms V and VI

Because of the close link between forms V–VI and II–III, you will find that many of the same rules apply to the irregular verbs in both cases.

Doubled verbs:
• Doubled verbs behave as regular verbs in form V (as for form II, doubling the middle root letter means that the second and third root letters of a doubled verb are always written separately.)
• Doubled verbs in form VI will follow the same rules as for the basic doubled verb (see page 30) but are rare and not worth too much attention.

Verbs with *hamza* as a root letter:
• Verbs with *hamza* behave roughly as regular verbs, but see rules about spelling on page 34. Because past and present verbs in forms V and VI are nearly always vowelized with *fatHas* (ˍ), you will usually see the *hamza* written on an *'alif* (أ).
• When *hamza* is the middle (second) root letter, it can be written by itself on the line in form VI (as in form III) because it follows a long vowel (see page 30).

Weak verbs:
• Verbs with *waaw* or *yaa'* as the first or second root letter (*assimilated* and *hollow* verbs) behave as *regular* verbs in forms V and VI, as they do in forms II and III.
• Verbs with *waaw* or *yaa'* as the third root (*defective*) behave irregularly in both forms. *Defective* verbs in forms V and VI are characterized by an *'alif maqsuura* at the end of both the past and present tenses — *aa* vowel written on a *yaa'* without dots, see Appendix (i). This is the same ending as the مشى basic group of verbs in the past tense, but like the ينسى group in the present tense (see pages 27–28).

	Form V (*yatafaɛɛal*)		Form VI (*yatafaaɛal*)	
Doubled verbs				
past	تَرَدَّدَ	hesitated	*no verbs in*	
present	يَتَرَدَّد	hesitates	*common circulation*	
Verbs with hamza				
as 1st root letter:				
past	تَأَثَّرَ	was influenced	تَآلَفَ	were familiar
present	يَتَأَثَّر	is influenced	يَتَآلَف	are familiar
as 2nd root letter:				
past	تَفَأَّلَ	was optimistic	تَسَاءَلَ	wondered
present	يَتَفَأَّلَ	is optimistic	يَتَسَاءَل	wonders
as 3nd root letter:				
past	تَنَبَّأَ	predicted	تَكَافَأَ	were equal
present	يَتَنَبَّأَ	predicts	يَتَكَافَأَ	are equal
Weak verbs				
assimilated:				
past	تَوَقَّعَ	expected	تَوَافَقَ	agreed together
present	يَتَوَقَّع	expects	يَتَوَافَق	agree together
hollow:				
past	تَلَوَّنَ	was colored (in)	تَعَاوَنَ	cooperated
present	يَتَلَوَّن	is colored (in)	يَتَعَاوَن	cooperate
defective:				
past	تَمَنَّى	wished/wanted	تَلَاقَى	met together
present	يَتَمَنَّى	wishes/wants	يَتَلَاقَى	meet together

Summary of forms V–VI

- Form V and VI verbs are characterized by the ـتَ (*ta*) in front of the root letters.

- Like form II, form V verbs also double the middle root letter (يَتَفَعَّل – *yatafaɛɛal*).

- Like form III, form VI verbs also add a long *aa* after the first root letter (يَتَفاعَل – *yatafaaɛal*).

- Form V and VI verbs are vowelized throughout with *fatHa* (ـَ) in the past and present tenses.

- Forms V and VI can be the *reflexive* of forms II and III. Form VI often carries the meaning of "doing something together in a group."

- Verbs that are irregular in the basic form may also act irregularly in these derived forms (see table page 52).

10 Derived forms VII–X

The third group of derived forms is made of up forms VII (يَنْفَعِل – *yanfaɛ il*), VIII (يَفْتَعِل – *yaftaɛ il*), and X (يَسْتَفْعِل – *yastafɛ il*). Form IX (characterized by doubling the final root letter) has virtually died out in modern Arabic. The only context in which you might see it is connected with changing color, e.g.: يَحْمَرّ (*yaHmarr*) – "turn red" or "blush," etc.

Characteristics

Past tense

- Form VII is made by adding *in* (اِنْ) in front of the root letters:

  فَعَلَ (basic verb *faɛ ala*) ➞ اِنْفَعَلَ (form VII verb *infaɛ ala*)

- Form VIII is made by adding *i* (اِ) in front of the first root letter and *taa'* (ت) after it:

  فَعَلَ (basic verb *faɛ ala*) ➞ اِفْتَعَلَ (form VIII verb *iftaɛ ala*)

- Form X is formed by adding an *ista* (اِسْتَ) in front of the root letters and putting a *sukuun* over the first root letter:

  فَعَلَ (basic verb *faɛ ala*) ➞ اِسْتَفْعَلَ (form VIII verb *istafɛ ala*)

Present tense

In the present tense, these three forms keep the same basic features of the past tense but are vowelized differently. They all have a *fatHa* (ـَ) as the first two vowels and a *kasra* (ـِ) as the third:

Form VII: يَنْفَعِل (*yanfaɛil*)

Form VIII: يَفْتَعِل (*yaftaɛil*)

Form X: يَسْتَفْعِل (*yastafɛil*)

Other characteristics

- The *kasra* (*i*) that begins the past tense of all these three forms will disappear (elide) if the word before <u>ends</u> with a vowel. This is because the *kasra* is carried by *hamzat al waSl* – see Appendix (i).

اِنْقَلَبَ مَرْكَبُهُ. (*inqalaba markabuhu*) – His boat turned over.

but

ثُمَّ اِنْقَلَبَ مَرْكَبُهُ. (*thumma <u>n</u>qalaba markabuhu*) – Then his boat turned over.

- Form VII is almost never formed with verbs whose first root letter is *hamza* (ء), *waaw* (و), *yaa'* (ي), *nuun* (ن), *lam* (ل), or *ra'* (ر). The combination of sounds would be unnatural in Arabic.

- The first root letter can affect the beginning of Form VIII verbs. These can seem complicated but follow these general rules:
  - When the first root letter is *taa'* (ت), *waaw* (و) or *hamza* (ء), this is replaced by a doubling of the *taa'* at the beginning of the pattern:

    اِتَّخَذَ/يَتَّخِذ (*ittakhadha/yattakhidh*: "to adopt") – from the root: أخذ

    اِتَّفَقَ/يَتَّفِق (*ittafaqa/yattafiq*: "to agree") – from the root: وفق

  - When the first root letter is *daal* (د), *dhaal* (ذ) or *zaay* (ز), the *taa'* at the beginning of form VIII is replaced by a *daal*. In the case of *daal* and *dhaal*, this is then usually combined with the first root letter to produce a double *daal*:

    اِزْدَحَمَ/يَزْدَحِم (*izdaHama/yazdaHim*: "to crowd") – from the root: زحم

    اِدَّخَرَ/يَدَّخِر (*iddakhkhara/yaddakhkhir*: "to save/store") – from: ذخر

  - When the first root letter is *Taa'* (ط), *Zaa'* (ظ), *Saad* (ص) or *Daad* (ض), the *taa'* at the beginning of form VIII is replaced by a *Taa'*. In the case of *Taa'* and *Zaa'*, this is then usually combined with the first root letter to produce a double *Taa'*:

اِضْطَرَبَ/يَضْطَرِب (iDTaraba/yaDTarib: "to be disturbed") – from: ضرب

اِطَّلَعَ/يَطَّلِع (iTTalaعa/yaTTaliع : "to be informed about") – from: طلع

Common meaning patterns

1. Form VII is relatively uncommon and usually has a passive meaning:

يَقْلِب (basic verb *yaqlib* – to overturn/turn [something] over)➡

يَنْقَلِب (form VII verb *yanqalib* – to be overturned)

يَكْسَر (basic verb *yaksar* – to break)➡

يَنْكَسِر (form VII verb *yankasir* – to be broken)

2. Form VIII is a common form and is usually intransitive, but there is no consistent meaning pattern connected with it. These verbs are often close to the basic root meaning:

يَجْمَع (basic verb *yajmaع* – to gather/put together)➡

يَجْتَمِع (form VIII verb *yajtamiع* – to assemble/meet together)

يَقْرُب (basic verb *yaqrub* – to be near)➡

يَقْتَرِب (form VIII verb *yaqtarib* – to approach/advance)

يَنْشُر (basic verb *yanshur* – to publish/diffuse)➡

يَنْتَشِر (form VIII verb *yantashir* – to become widespread)

3. Form X often has the meaning of <u>asking</u> for something:

يَأْذَن (basic verb *ya'dhan* – to permit)➡

يَسْتَأْذِن (form X verb *yasta'dhin* – to ask for permission)

يَعْلَم (basic verb *yaع lam* – to know)➡

يَسْتَعْلِم (form X verb *yastaع lim* – to inquire ["ask for knowledge"])

4. Form X can also mean to "consider or find something …":

يَحْسُن (basic verb *yaHsun* – to be beautiful)➤

يَسْتَحْسِن (form X verb *yastaHsin* – to admire ["consider beautiful"])

Here is a table showing the past and present tenses for these three verb forms, followed by some example sentences:

Past

singular		Form VII (infaɛala)		Form VIII (iftaɛala)		Form X (istafɛala)
أَنا	اِنْقَلَبْتُ	(inqalabtu)	اِقْتَرَبْتُ	(iqtarabtu)	اِسْتَعْلَمْتُ	(istaɛlamtu)
أَنْتَ	اِنْقَلَبْتَ	(inqalabta)	اِقْتَرَبْتَ	(iqtarabta)	اِسْتَعْلَمْتَ	(istaɛlamta)
أَنْتِ	اِنْقَلَبْتِ	(inqalabti)	اِقْتَرَبْتِ	(iqtarabti)	اِسْتَعْلَمْتِ	(istaɛlamti)
هُوَ	اِنْقَلَبَ	(inqalaba)	اِقْتَرَبَ	(iqtaraba)	اِسْتَعْلَمَ	(istaɛlama)
هِيَ	اِنْقَلَبَتْ	(inqalabat)	اِقْتَرَبَتْ	(iqtarabat)	اِسْتَعْلَمَتْ	(istaɛlamat)

plural

		Form VII		Form VIII		Form X
نَحْنُ	اِنْقَلَبْنا	(inqalabnaa)	اِقْتَرَبْنا	(iqtarabnaa)	اِسْتَعْلَمْنا	(istaɛlamnaa)
أَنْتُمْ	اِنْقَلَبْتُمْ	(inqalabtum)	اِقْتَرَبْتُمْ	(iqtarabtum)	اِسْتَعْلَمْتُمْ	(istaɛlamtum)
أَنْتُنَّ	اِنْقَلَبْتُنَّ	(inqalabtunna)	اِقْتَرَبْتُنَّ	(iqtarabtunna)	اِسْتَعْلَمْتُنَّ	(istaɛlamtunna)
هُم	اِنْقَلَبُوا	(inqalabuu)	اِقْتَرَبُوا	(iqtarabuu)	اِسْتَعْلَمُوا	(istaɛlamuu)
هُنَّ	اِنْقَلَبْنَ	(inqalabna)	اِقْتَرَبْنَ	(iqtarabna)	اِسْتَعْلَمْنَ	(istaɛlamna)

Present

singular	Form VII (yanfaع il)		Form VIII (yaftaع il)		Form X (yastafع il)	
أنا	أَنْقَلِب	('anqalib[u])	أَقْتَرِب	('aqtarib[u])	أَسْتَعْلِم	('astaع lim[u])
أَنْتَ	تَنْقَلِب	(tanqalib[u])	تَقْتَرِب	(taqtarib[u])	تَسْتَعْلِم	(tastaع lim[u])
أَنْتِ	تَنْقَلِبِينَ	(tanqalibiina)	تَقْتَرِبِينَ	(taqtaribiina)	تَسْتَعْلِمِينَ	(tastaع limiina)
هُوَ	يَنْقَلِب	(yanqalib[u])	يَقْتَرِب	(yaqtarib[u])	يَسْتَعْلِم	(yastaع lim[u])
هِيَ	تَنْقَلِب	(tanqalib[u])	تَقْتَرِب	(taqtarib[u])	تَسْتَعْلِم	(tastaع lim[u])

plural

	Form VII		Form VIII		Form X	
نَحْنُ	نَنْقَلِب	(nanqalib[u])	نَقْتَرِب	(naqtarib[u])	نَسْتَعْلِم	(nastaع lim[u])
أَنْتُمْ	تَنْقَلِبُونَ	(tanqalibuuna)	تَقْتَرِبُونَ	(taqtaribuuna)	تَسْتَعْلِمُونَ	(tastaع limuuna)
أَنْتُنَّ	تَنْقَلِبْنَ	(tanqalibna)	تَقْتَرِبْنَ	(taqtaribna)	تَسْتَعْلِمْنَ	(tastaع limna)
هُم	يَنْقَلِبُونَ	(yanqalibuuna)	يَقْتَرِبُونَ	(yaqtaribuuna)	يَسْتَعْلِمُونَ	(yastaع limuuna)
هُنَّ	يَنْقَلِبْنَ	(yanqalibna)	يَقْتَرِبْنَ	(yaqtaribna)	يَسْتَعْلِمْنَ	(yastaع limna)

اِنْقَلَبَت السَّفِينة في العاصِفة.

The ship capsized in the storm.

شَعَرْنا بالحَرارة حَيْنَ اقْتَرَبْنا مِن الفُرْن.

We felt the heat when we approached the oven.

يَسْتَعْلِم السائِح من الدَليل عَنْ مكان الأهْرام.

The tourist asks the guide about the location of the pyramids.

اِنْقَسَمَت البيتْزا إلى أرْبَعة أجْزاء.

The pizza was divided into four pieces.

اِسْتَخْرَجَ الجَرَّاح الرُّصاصة مِن كِتْفِي.

The surgeon removed the bullet from my shoulder.

Irregular verbs in forms VII–X

Here are some notes about how irregular verbs behave in forms VII–X, followed by a summary table:

Doubled verbs:
• Doubled verbs in forms VII, VIII, and X follow the same rules as for the basic doubled verb (see page 30).

Verbs with *hamza* as a root letter:
• Verbs with *hamza* are not common in forms VII–X. When they do occur, they behave roughly as *regular* verbs, but see rules about spelling on page 34. Note in particular that form VIII verbs with *hamza* as the first letter behave like assimilated verbs (see table).

Weak verbs:
• *Assimilated* verbs are virtually nonexistent in form VII and regular in form X. In form VIII, the first letter drops out and is replaced by a doubling of the *taa'*.
• *Hollow* verbs in forms VII–X behave similarly to basic hollow verbs. They have a long vowel at the end if there is no *sukuun* over the third root letter. Notice that this long vowel is usually an *aa* sound (ﺎﻟ). Only in the present tense of form X is it an *ii* sound (ﻲ). If the third root letter has a *sukuun* over it, the long vowel will become short. For example, "he resigned" = اِسْتَقَال (*istaqaala*), but "I resigned" = اِسْتَقَلْتُ (*istaqaltu*).
• Verbs with *waaw* or *yaa'* as the third root (*defective*) behave irregularly in forms VII, VIII, and X and have the same endings as the يمشي/مشى basic group of verbs (see pages 27–28).

	Form VII (*yanfaعil*)	**Form VIII** (*yaftaعil*)	**Form X** (*yastafعil*)
Doubled verbs			
past	اِنْضَمَّ joined (club)	اِمْتَدَّ extended	اِسْتَمَرَّ continued
present	يَنْضَمّ joins (club)	يَمْتَدّ extend	يَسْتَمِرّ continues
Verbs with hamza			
as 1st root letter:			
past	*no verbs in*	اِتَّخَذَ adopted	اِسْتَأْجَرَ rented
present	*common circulation*	يَتَّخِذ adopt	يَسْتَأْجِر rents
as 2nd root letter:			
past	*no verbs in*	اِبْتَأَسَ was sad	*no verbs in*
present	*common circulation*	يَبْتَئِس is sad	*common circulation*
as 3nd root letter:			
past	اِنْقَرَأ was read	اِبْتَدَأ began	اِسْتَهْزَأ mocked
present	يَنْقَرِئ is read	يَبْتَدِئ begins	يَسْتَهْزِئ mocks
Weak verbs			
assimilated:			
past	*no verbs in*	اِتَّفَقَ agreed	اِسْتَوْقَفَ stopped
present	*common circulation*	يَتَّفِق agrees	يَسْتَوْقِف stops
hollow:			
past	اِنْقادَ was led	اِحْتاجَ needed	اِسْتَقالَ resigned
present	يَنْقاد is led	يَحْتاج needs	يَسْتَقيل resigns
defective:			
past	اِنْحَنَى bowed, bent	اِشْتَرَى bought	اِسْتَثْنَى excluded
present	يَنْحَني bows, bends	يَشْتَري buys	يَسْتَثْني excludes

Summary of forms VII–X

- Form VII verbs are characterized by the *nuun* (ن) before the root letters (يَنْفَعِل – *yanfaε il*).

- Form VIII verbs are characterized by the *taa'* (ت) after the first root letter (يَفْتَعِل – *yaftaε il*). This form can change somewhat depending on the first root letter.

- Form X verbs are characterized by the *siin* (س) and *taa'* (ت) – or *sta* sound – before the root letters (يَسْتَفْعِل – *yastafε il*).

- In the past tense, forms VII–X start with *i* (ا): *infaε ala, iftaε ala, istafε ala.*

- In the present tense, forms VII–X are vowelled with 2 *fatHas* and a *kasra*: *yanfaε il, yaftaε il, yastafε il.*

- Form VII often has a *passive* meaning.

- Form VIII is a common form but has no consistent meaning patterns associated with it.

- Form X has two common meaning patterns: to think or consider that something is (beautiful, etc.), and to ask for something.

11 Essentials of making sentences with verbs

The first chapters of this book have covered the essentials of Arabic verbs — the basic tenses and forms. Before we move on to look at some of the more detailed aspects of how verbs are used, we need to recap and expand on how to use verbs in sentences.

Some information on how verbs behave in sentences has already been presented in the first ten verb chapters. Below is a summary of this information with important additional notes.

- Arabic verbs change according to the *subject* (who/what is carrying out the action):

  كَتَبَ خالِد رِسالة لِلوَزير. Khalid wrote (*kataba*) a letter to the minister.

  كَتَبَتْ فاطمة رِسالة لِلوَزير. Fatma wrote (*katabat*) a letter to the minister.

- If the subject is a mixed group of male and female people, the <u>masculine</u> is used:

  الأوْلاد والبَنات دَخَلُوا المَدْرَسة. The boys and girls entered the school.

  There are different dual forms for two people or things. These are covered in Chapter 18 (for verbs) and Chapter 28 (in general).

- Because the *prefixes* and *suffixes* (letters on the beginning and end of the verb) tell you the subject, Arabic does not often use personal pronouns with verbs (e.g., أنا – "I," هُوَ – "he," etc.). If they are used, it is usually for emphasis after the verb:

  دَخَل أخي جامِعة القاهِرة في عام ٢٠٠٥، ثُمَّ بَعدَ سَنتَيْن دَخَلْتُ أنا.
  My brother attended Cairo University in 2005, then two years later I [too] attended.

- The verb can come before or after the subject. This is largely a matter of emphasis/level of formality. If a sentence starts with the subject, you might see the word إنَّ ('*inna*) first. This word is added for emphasis but has no direct translation:

كَتَبَ خَالِد رِسالة لِلوَزير. (verb before subject)

إنَّ خَالِدًا كَتَبَ رِسالة لِلوَزير. (subject before verb with إنَّ)

إنَّ is followed by the accusative case (خَالِدًا – *khaalidan*) – see Appendix (ii).

- The plural verbs are only used for people. If the subject of a verb is plural but <u>not human</u> (i.e., three or more things/ideas, etc.), Arabic grammar regards this as <u>feminine singular</u> (refer to Chapter 21 if you need to review this concept). This means you have to use the هِيَ ("she") part of the verb:

وَقَعَت الصُّحُون عَلَى الأَرْض وانْكَسَرَت. The plates fell on the floor and broke.

إنَّ الدُوَل الإسْلاميَّة تَتَعاوَن مِنْ أَجْل السلام. The Islamic states are cooperating for [the sake of] peace.

This is a very important aspect of Arabic grammar generally since there is virtually no exception to the rule. It might seem odd to you to refer to a group of plates or countries as "she", but it will seem just as odd to an Arabic speaker if you use the plural forms which they reserve for people.

- If the subject is a group of people, the verb will still be singular if it comes <u>before</u> the subject. It will only change according to whether the subject is masculine or feminine:

وَصَلَ الرِجال إلَى المَصْنع. The men arrived at the factory.

بَدَأَت السَيِّدات اجْتِماعهُنّ. The women began their meeting.

Look at the next sentences. They have two verbs, before and after the subject:

حَضَرَ المُدَرِّسون اجْتِماعاً واتَّفَقُوا عَلَى البَرْنامِج لِلعام القادِم.
The teachers attended a meeting and agreed on the program
for the upcoming year.

كَتَبَت البَنات خِطابات، ثُمَّ خَرَجْنَ.
The girls wrote letters and then went out.

The subject of the first sentence above is <u>masculine plural</u> (*mudarrisuuna* – teachers). The first verb (*HaDara* – attended) is in the masculine singular because it comes before the subject. The second verb (*ittafaquu* – agreed) has the plural ending *uu* since it comes after the subject. The same is true of the second sentence, except that the subject is now <u>feminine plural</u> (*banaat* – girls) and so the feminine singular ending *at* (*katabat* – wrote) and feminine plural ending *na* (*kharajna* – went out) are used.

These are the basic guidelines for using verbs. You will become more aware of subtle style differences through reading and absorbing Arabic that is written in a natural style by native speakers.

12 Verbs in the subjunctive

In previous chapters, we have seen how different verbs work in the standard present tense. Now we need to look at some variations that can occur to the present verb in certain situations. Grammarians often call these variations "moods of the verb." The two moods you need to know in Arabic are the *subjunctive* and the *jussive*. Only in the minority of cases do these moods affect the way a verb is written or pronounced. However, you do need to know the whole story, otherwise you cannot understand or work out the changes that occur in this significant minority of cases.

The individual usages of the subjunctive and jussive listed in the next two chapters are relatively limited and easy to remember. You will soon come to connect them with particular words and phrases.

Regular verbs in the subjunctive

In regular verbs, the subjunctive is very similar to the standard present tense. This is also true of the derived forms.

The most significant change is that when the standard present tense ends in a *nuun* (ن), this is dropped in the *subjunctive*. This affects the masculine plurals – هُم (*hum*) and أَنْتُم ('*antum*) – and the feminine أَنْتِ ('*anti*) parts of the verb. (The dual is also affected – see Chapter 28). These changes affect the spelling and pronunciation.

Less significantly, the final (often unpronounced) *Damma* (ـُ) that ends many parts of the standard present tense (see page 15) changes to a *fatHa* (ـَ) in the subjunctive. In other words يَكْتُبُ (*yaktubu*) becomes

يَكْتُبَ (*yaktuba*). As both these alternatives are usually written without vowels and pronounced يَكْتُب (*yaktub*), you would not normally notice the change.

The table below shows the standard present tense and the subjunctive for the regular verb *yaktub* (to write):

		Standard present	**Subjunctive**
singular			
أَنا	I	أَكْتُبُ 'aktub(u)	أَكْتُبَ 'aktub(a)
أَنْتَ	you (masc.)	تَكْتُبُ taktub(u)	تَكْتُبَ taktub(a)
أَنْتِ	you (fem.)	تَكْتُبِينَ taktubiina	تَكْتُبِي taktubii
هُوَ	he/it	يَكْتُبُ yaktub(u)	يَكْتُبَ yaktub(a)
هِيَ	she/it	تَكْتُبُ taktub(u)	تَكْتُبَ taktub(a)
plural			
نَحْنُ	we	نَكْتُبُ naktub(u)	نَكْتُبَ naktub(a)
أَنْتُمْ	you (masc. pl)	تَكْتُبُونَ taktubuuna	*تَكْتُبُوا taktubuu
أَنْتُنَّ	you (fem. pl)	تَكْتُبْنَ taktubna	تَكْتُبْنَ taktubna
هُم	they (masc.)	يَكْتُبُونَ yaktubuuna	*يَكْتُبُوا yaktubuu
هُنَّ	they (fem.)	يَكْتُبْنَ yaktubna	يَكْتُبْنَ yaktubna

*Notice that the the masculine plurals have an extra *'alif* in the subjunctive. As with the past tense (see page 14), this *'alif* is silent.

Irregular verbs in the subjunctive

Irregular verbs do not stray much from the rules for regular verbs in the subjunctive. There are some minor differences which you may meet occasionally:

- Weak verbs that end in a long *ii* (ـِي) or *uu* (ـُو) in the standard present tense, will end in *iya* (ـِيَ) or *uwa* (ـُوَ) in the subjunctive (if fully pronounced), but those that end in a long *aa* (ـَى) do not change:

  يَنْتَهِي *yantahii* – to finish – standard present tense →
  يَنْتَهِيَ *yantahiya* – subjunctive

  يَبْدُو *yabduu* – to seem/appear – standard present tense →
  يَبْدُوَ *yabduwa* – subjunctive

  يَنْسَى *yansaa* – to forget – standard present tense →
  يَنْسَى *yansaa* – subjunctive (no change)

Uses of the subjunctive

The subjunctive is only used when verbs come after particular words (or "particles" as they are sometimes called). The most common of these is أَنْ (*'an* – to). Here is a fuller list, in rough order of frequency:

أَنْ	*'an*	to
(ألّا)	(*'allaa*	not to)
لِ	*li*	to/in order to
لَنْ	*lan*	shall/will not (used to make the future negative)
حَتَّى	*Hatta**	so that
لِكَيْ	*likayy*	in order to

* *Hatta* also means "until." The subjunctive is only used when it means "so that."

The structure أَنْ (*'an*) + *subjunctive* is used frequently in Arabic, often after verbs where in English we would use the infinitive (e.g., "can't run" or "want to vote").

لا أَسْتَطِيع أَنْ أَجْرِيَ مَعَكُم اليَوْم لأَنِّي مَرِيض.

I can't run with you today because I'm sick.

هَلْ تُرِيدونَ أَنْ تُصَوِّتُوا في الاِنْتِخابات؟

Do you [plural] want to vote in the elections?

The other particles are used in roughly the same contexts as they would be in English:

عَلَيْكِ أن تُذاكِرِي لِتَنْجَحِي في الاِمْتِحان.

You [feminine] should study [lit: "on you that you study"]
in order to pass the exam.

هَيَا نَأْكُل الآن حَتَى نَنْتَهِيَ قَبْلَ بِداية البَرْنامِج.

Let's eat now so that we can finish before the start of the program.

لَنْ تَرَى القَمَر بِالنَهار.

You won't see the moon in the daytime.

اِشْتَرَيْتُ تَذكِرتي مِن الاِنترَنت لِكَيْ أُوَفِّرَ في سِعرِها.

I bought my ticket from the Internet in order to save on its cost.

Summary of the *subjunctive*

- The *subjunctive* is a variation ("mood") of the present tense used after certain words.

- The most common of these words is أَنْ (*'an* – to).

- The *subjunctive* is very similar to the standard present tense for both regular and irregular verbs.

- The major difference affecting everyday usage and spelling is that the *nuun* (ن) is dropped from the end of the masculine plurals – يَكْتُبُوا (*yaktubuu*)/تَكْتُبُوا (*taktubuu*) – and the feminine "you" – تَكْتُبِي (*taktubii*).

13 Verbs in the jussive (incl. the imperative)

The jussive is the second variation of the present tense that you need to know. In many ways it is more important than the subjunctive, partly because it is more frequently used and partly because it displays more irregularities.

Regular verbs in the jussive

In regular verbs, the jussive, like the subjunctive, is very similar to the standard present tense. Again like the subjunctive, the most significant change in regular verbs is that the *nuun* (ن) is dropped at the end of the parts of the verb for masculine plurals "they" هُم (*hum*) and "you" أَنْتُم (*'antum*), and the feminine singular "you" أَنْتِ (*'anti*). (The dual is also affected — see Chapter 28).

The difference in regular verbs between the subjunctive and the jussive is that the *Damma* (ـُ) that ends many parts of the standard present tense (see page 15) changes to a *sukuun* (ـْ) in the jussive, rather than the *fatHa* (ـَ) of the subjunctive. In other words يَكْتُبُ (*yaktubu*) becomes يَكْتُبْ (*yaktub*) in the jussive. Since the standard present tense, the subjunctive and the jussive are all often written without vowels and pronounced يَكْتُب (*yaktub*), you would not normally notice this change in regular verbs. (But it does become significant in irregular verbs — see the section on page 70.)

The table on the next page shows the standard present tense and the jussive for the regular verb يَكْتُب *yaktub* (to write):

	Standard present	**Jussive**
singular		
أَنا I	أَكْتُبُ 'aktub(u)	أَكْتُبْ 'aktub
أَنْتَ you (masc.)	تَكْتُبُ taktub(u)	تَكْتُبْ taktub
أَنْتِ you (fem.)	تَكْتُبِينَ taktubiina	تَكْتُبِي taktubii
هُوَ he/it	يَكْتُبُ yaktub(u)	يَكْتُبْ yaktub
هِيَ she/it	تَكْتُبُ taktub(u)	تَكْتُبْ taktub
plural		
نَحْنُ we	نَكْتُبُ naktub(u)	نَكْتُبْ naktub
أَنْتُمْ you (masc. pl)	تَكْتُبُونَ taktubuuna	تَكْتُبُوا* taktubuu
أَنْتُنَّ you (fem. pl)	تَكْتُبْنَ taktubna	تَكْتُبْنَ taktubna
هُم they (masc.)	يَكْتُبُونَ yaktubuuna	يَكْتُبُوا* yaktubuu
هُنَّ they (fem.)	يَكْتُبْنَ yaktubna	يَكْتُبْنَ yaktubna

*Notice that the the masculine plurals have an extra 'alif in the jussive as they do in the subjunctive. As with the past tense (see page 14), this 'alif is silent.

Irregular verbs in the *jussive*

The fact that the jussive ends in a *sukuun*, although largely insignificant in regular verbs, does have a big impact on many types of irregular verbs. Because the jussive replaces the *Damma* over the third root letter of many parts of the present tense with a *sukuun*, this can fundamentally affect the whole formation of many irregular verbs. The easiest way to approach this is to take each type of irregular verb in turn, as follows:

Verbs with waaw or yaa' as a root letter

- Verbs with waaw or yaa' as the first root letter *(assimilated verbs)* follow the same rules as regular verbs:

  يَصِلُ *yaSil(u)* – he arrives (standard present tense)

  يَصِلْ *yaSil* – he arrives (jussive)

- Verbs with *waaw* or *yaa'* as the second root letter *(hollow verbs)* change significantly in the jussive. These changes affect both the pronunciation and the spelling and so it is important to understand them. Firstly, remind yourself of the basic rules for hollow verbs (see pages 22–26 if you need more help):

> - **Sukuun** over third root letter of regular verb = **short vowel** in the middle of irregular hollow verb
> - **Vowel** over third root letter of regular verb = **long vowel** in the middle of irregular hollow verb

You know that a hollow verb in the standard present tense usually has a long vowel in the middle because the third root letter has a vowel over it — for example, يَزُورُ (*yazuur(u)* – he visits). In the jussive, however, the third root letter has a *sukuun* over it, and this means that a hollow verb will have a <u>short</u> vowel in the middle: يَزُرْ (*yazur*). Look at the table below showing how this rule applies to the other parts of the verb يزور . You could try covering the right-hand column and predicting the jussive by looking at the rules above.

		Standard present	**Jussive**
singular			
أَنَا I		أَزُورُ 'azuur(u)	أَزُرْ 'azur
أَنْتَ you (masc.)		تَزُورُ tazuur(u)	تَزُرْ tazur
أَنْتِ you (fem.)		تَزُورِينَ tazuuriina	تَزُورِي tazurii
هُوَ he/it		يَزُورُ yazuur(u)	يَزُرْ yazur
هِيَ she/it		تَزُورُ tazuur(u)	تَزُرْ tazur

	Standard present	**Jussive**
plural		
نَحْنُ we	نَزُورُ nazuur(u)	نَزُرْ nazur
أَنْتُمْ you (masc. pl)	تَزُورُونَ tazuuruuna	تَزُورُوا tazuuruu
أَنْتُنَّ you (fem. pl)	تَزُرْنَ tazurna	تَزُرْنَ tazurna
هُم they (masc.)	يَزُورُونَ yazuuruuna	يَزُورُوا yazuuruu
هُنَّ they (fem.)	يَزُرْنَ yazurna	يَزُرْنَ yazurna

Notice that the feminine plurals are the only parts of the present tense that remain the same in the jussive. You can apply the pattern above to all hollow verbs, except that the short vowel will be *fatHa* (ـَ) if there is a long *aa* (ـَا) in the standard present tense and *kasra* (ـِ) if there is a long *ii* (ـِي):

يَبِيعُ *yabii*ε*(u)* – to sell – standard present tense →
يَبِعْ *yabi*ε – jussive

يَنَامُ *yanaam(u)* – to sleep – standard present tense →
يَنَمْ *yanam* – jussive

يُرِيدُ *yuriid(u)* – to want – standard present tense →
يُرِدْ *yurid* – jussive

• Verbs with *waaw* or *yaa'* as the third root letter (*defective verbs*) also change significantly in the jussive. These verbs often have a long vowel at the end of the standard present tense (see pages 28–29). This changes to a short vowel in the jussive. Defective verbs in the jussive can be awkward to spot since they often look as if they only have two root letters, especially if you see them without vowels. Look at the standard present tense and the jussive for the verb يَمْشِي (*yamshii* – to walk):

	Standard present	**Jussive**
singular		
أَنَا I	أَمْشِي 'amshii	أَمْشِ 'amshi
أَنْتَ you (masc.)	تَمْشِي tamshii	تَمْشِ tamshi
أَنْتِ you (fem.)	تَمْشِينَ tamshiina	تَمْشِي tamshii
هُوَ he/it	يَمْشِي yamshii	يَمْشِ yamshi
هِيَ she/it	تَمْشِي tamshii	تَمْشِ tamshi
plural		
نَحْنُ we	نَمْشِي namshii	نَمْشِ namshi
أَنْتُمْ you (masc. pl)	تَمْشُونَ tamshuuna	تَمْشُوا tamshuu
أَنْتُنَّ you (fem. pl)	تَمْشِينَ tamshiina	تَمْشِينَ tamshiina
هُم they (masc.)	يَمْشُونَ yamshuuna	يَمْشُوا yamshuu
هُنَّ they (fem.)	يَمْشِينَ yamshiina	يَمْشِينَ yamshiina

As with hollow verbs, the short vowel in the jussive of defective verbs depends on the original long vowel:

يَنْتَهِي *yantahii* – to finish – standard present tense →
يَنْتَهِ *yantahi* – jussive

يَشْكُو *yashkuu* – to complain – standard present tense →
يَشْكُ *yashku* – jussive

يَنْسَى *yansaa* – to forget – standard present tense →
يَنْسَ *yansa* – jussive

Doubled verbs

• The rule affecting whether the identical root letters are written separately or together in a doubled verb is connected with the vowel

over the <u>third</u> root letter in a regular verb. Remind yourself of the rule
(see also Chapter 5):

> • **Sukuun** over third root letter of regular verb =
>   second and third root letters **written separately** in doubled verb
> • **Vowel** over third root letter of regular verb =
>   second and third root letters **written together** in doubled verb

The *sukuun* that characterizes much of the jussive means that the
second and third root letters are written separately more often than in
the standard present tense. Try covering the right-hand column of the
table below and predicting the jussive for the doubled verb يَرُدّ
(*yarudd* – to reply), applying the rules above.

		Standard present	**Jussive**
singular			
أَنا	I	أَرُدُّ ’arudd(u)	أَرْدُدْ ’ardud
أَنْتَ	you (masc.)	تَرُدُّ tarudd(u)	تَرْدُدْ tardud
أَنْتِ	you (fem.)	تَرُدِّينَ taruddiina	تَرُدِّي taruddii
هُوَ	he/it	يَرُدُّ yarudd(u)	يَرْدُدْ yardud
هِيَ	she/it	تَرُدُّ tarudd(u)	تَرْدُدْ tardud
plural			
نَحْنُ	we	نَرُدُّ narudd(u)	نَرْدُدْ nardud
أَنْتُمْ	you (masc. pl)	تَرُدُّونَ tarudduuna	تَرُدُّوا tarudduu
أَنْتُنَّ	you (fem. pl)	تَرْدُدْنَ tardudna	تَرْدُدْنَ tardudna
هُم	they (masc.)	يَرُدُّونَ yardduuna	يَرُدُّوا yardduu
هُنَّ	they (fem.)	يَرْدُدْنَ yardudna	يَرْدُدْنَ yardudna

Verbs with *hamza* as a root letter

• These verbs do not vary from regular verbs in the jussive. However, you should be aware of an alternative for the commonly used verb يَسْأَل (*yas'al* – to ask):

يَسْأَلُ *yas'al(u)* – to ask – standard present tense →

يَسْأَل *yas'al* or يَسَل *yasal* – jussive

Uses of the jussive

The jussive has three main uses in modern Arabic.

Negative commands

The jussive is used after لا (*laa*) to mean "don't" as an order or command:

لا تَزُرْ مَريضَك لأَكْثَر مِن نِصْف ساعة.

Don't visit your patient for more than half an hour.

لا تُحاوِلوا أَنْ تَتَسَلَّقوا هذِهِ الشَّجَرة العالية.

Don't [*plural*] try to climb this tall tree.

fal (...فَـ) and li (...لِـ)

The jussive is used after ...فَـ (*fal*), or less commonly ...لِـ (*li*), with the meaning of "(so) let's:"

سَرَقَ اللُّصوص سَيارَتنا! فَلْنَذْهَبْ إلى الشُّرْطة.

Thieves have stolen our car! So let's go to the police.

فَلْنَطْلُبْ مِن جيرانِنا أَنْ يَمْتَنِعوا عَنْ قَرْع الطُّبول.

Let's ask our neighbors to stop banging drums.

Negative past

The jussive is used after لَمْ (*lam*) to make the past tense negative ("didn't"):

لَمْ أَتَزَوَّجْ بَعْد لأَنَّني مُفْلِس.
I haven't gotten married yet because I'm broke.

تَأَخَّرَتْ عَمَّتي لأَنَّها لَمْ تَعْثُرْ عَلى تاكسي.
My aunt was late because she didn't find a taxi.

لَمْ يَنْتَهِ المُدير المالي مِنْ تَقْريرِهِ قَبْلَ الاجْتِماع.
The finance manager didn't finish his report before the meeting.

The imperative

The jussive is also used as a base for forming the imperative, or
commands. There are two basic categories and almost all Arabic verbs
follow the rules for the appropriate category.

Verbs with *sukuun* over the first root letter

If a verb has a *sukuun* over the first root letter in the jussive, the letters
at the beginning (*prefix*) are taken off and replaced by an *'alif*:

تَكْتُب *(jussive – "you write")*

اكْتُب *(imperative – "Write!")*

In a basic (form I) verb, the *'alif* on the front of the imperative will
have a *Damma* if the middle vowel of the present is also a *Damma*, and
a *kasra* if the middle vowel is either a *fatHa* or a *kasra*:

تَشْرَبْ *tashrab* – you drink *(jussive)* →
اِشْرَبْ *ishrab* – Drink! *(imperative)*

تَطْلُبُوا *taTlubuu* – you [plural] request *(jussive)* →
اُطْلُبُوا *uTlubuu* – Request! *(imperative)*

تَذْهَبِي *tadhhabii* – you [fem.] go *(jussive)* →
اِذْهَبِي *idhhabii* – Go! *(imperative)*

Derived forms IV, VII, VII, and X also have a *sukuun* over the first root letter in the jussive and so have the added *'alif*. Form IV has a *fatHa* over the *'alif* and forms VII, VIII, and X all have a *kasra*:

تُرْسِل *tursil* – you send (*jussive, form IV*) →
أَرْسِل *arsil* – Send! (*imperative*)

تَسْتَعْلِمِي *tastaəlimii* – you [fem.] inquire (*jussive, form X*) →
اِسْتَعْلِمِي *istaəlimii* – Inquire! (*imperative*)

تَنْتَهِ *tantahi* – you finish (*jussive, form VIII*) →
اِنْتَهِ *intahi* – Finish! (*imperative*)

تَقْتَرِبوا *taqtaribuu* – you [pl.] approach (*jussive, form VIII*) →
اِقْتَرِبوا *iqtaribuu* – Approach! (*imperative*)

Verbs with a vowel over the first root letter

Some verbs have a vowel over the first root letter of the jussive, rather than a sukuun. These type of verbs do not have the initial *'alif*:

تُسَخِّن (*jussive* – "you heat/warm up")

سَخِّن (*imperative* – "Heat!")

Form II, III, V, and VI verbs are all like this, as are many irregular verbs, such as hollow verbs, doubled verbs, and verbs with *waaw* as the first root letter:

تَقُل *taqul* – you say (*jussive, hollow verb*) →
قُل *qul* – Say! (*imperative*)

تَتَذَكَّر *tatadhakkar* – you remember (*jussive, form V*) →
تَذَكَّر *tadhakkar* – Remember! (*imperative*)

تَرُدِّي *taruddii* – you [fem.] reply (*jussive, doubled verb*) →
رُدِّي *ruddii* – Reply! (*imperative*)

تَتَعَاوَنوا *tataəaawanuu* – you [pl.] cooperate (*jussive, form VI*) →
تَعَاوَنوا *taəaawanuu* – Cooperate! (*imperative*)

Here are some example sentences using the imperative:

تَعاوَنوا مَعاً في بِناء المَدْرَسة الجَديدة.

Cooperate in building the new school.

اِذْهَبي إلى الشاطِئ واسْبَحي مَعَ أَصْدِقائِكِ.

Go [*fem.*] to the beach and swim with your friends.

اِشْرَب الشاي قَبْلَ أَنْ يَبْرَد.

Drink the tea before it gets cold.

اُكْتُبْ اِسْمَك وعُنْوانك هُنا بِخَطّ واضِح.

Write your name and address here in clear handwriting.

ساعِدْني مِن فَضْلك لأَنَّ هذا الصُّنْدوق ثَقيل.

Help me please because this box is heavy.

اِذْهَب إلى السوق واشْتَرِ لي بَعْضَ الفاكِهة.

Go to the market and buy me some fruit.

Summary of the *jussive*

- The jussive is a variation ("mood") of the present tense used after certain words.

- The most common of these words are ﻻ (*laa*) to mean "don't" as an order, and لَم (*lam*) to make the past tense negative ("didn't").

- The jussive is very similar to the subjunctive. The difference is that there is a *sukuun* over the final root letter: يَكْتُبْ (*yaktub*), rather than a *fatHa* as in the subjunctive.

- The *sukuun* of the jussive changes the way many <u>irregular</u> verbs are written and pronounced. These need to be studied individually.

- The imperative (for command or requests) is also formed from the jussive by removing the initial prefix. If this leaves a *sukuun* over the first letter, an *'alif* is added at the beginning.

14 Making verbs negative

This chapter contains a summary of how to make verbs negative. Some of these have been mentioned in previous chapters, but this summary will be a useful reference.

In English, we usually make verbs negative by adding the word "not," by itself or with another small helping word such as "do," "did," etc:

I walked → I did not walk.

I am going → I am not going.

I will find → I will not find.

I like → I do not like.

In Arabic, there are different ways of making a verb negative for different tenses. You need to remember each individually.

Present tense

This is the simplest negative to form. You add the word لا (*laa*) in front of the standard present verb:

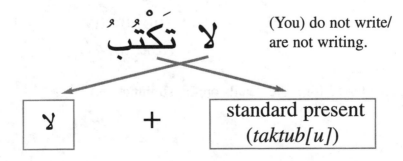

لا تَكْتُبُ   (You) do not write/ are not writing.

| لا | + | standard present (*taktub[u]*) |

Past tense

The negative of the past tense is formed with لَمْ (*lam*) + *jussive*:

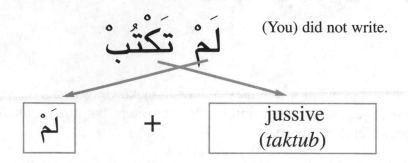

(You) did not write.

(See Chapter 13 for more details on the jussive.)

There is an alternative of the negative past tense formed by simply adding the word ما (*maa*) in front of the standard past: ما كَتَبْتَ (*maa katabta*). This is less common in modern written Arabic but is widespread in spoken dialects.

Future

The negative of the future is formed as follows:

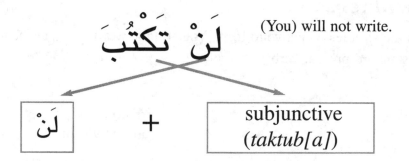

(You) will not write.

(See Chapter 12 for more details on the subjunctive.)

Imperative (commands)

This is formed by using لا followed by the *jussive*:

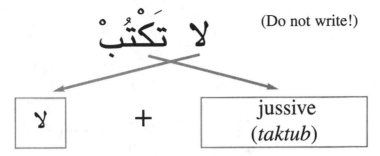

(Do not write!)

لا + جussive (*taktub*)

Be careful not to confuse this with the negative of the present tense.
Without the vowels, there will not always be a difference in the spelling,
but the context should tell you whether it is a command or not.

Here are some examples of the different negatives:

لا أُحِبُّ الاِسْتِحْمـام بالمـاء البـارد.
I don't like bathing with cold water.

لا تَلْعَبْ بالكَبْريت!
Don't play with matches!

كَلْبك لَنْ يَخونَك أَبَداً.
Your dog will never betray you.

لَمْ نَتَّفِقْ لأَنَّهُ كان هُنـاك فَرْقٌ بَيْنَ رَأينـا ورأيكُم.
We didn't agree because there was a difference between
our viewpoint and yours.

لا تُغَنِّ يا أَخي لأَنَّ صَوتك مُزْعِج.
Don't sing ["O Brother"] because your voice is irritating.

النَّعامة طائِرٌ لا يَطيرُ.
The ostrich is a bird [that] doesn't fly.

لَنْ تَنْتَهِيَ فِترة الجَفاف إنْ لَمْ يَنْزِلْ* المَطَر.
The period of dry weather won't end if the rain doesn't* fall.

* After إنْ (if) Arabic uses the <u>past</u> tense.

15 Making verbs passive

Before we talk about the passive in Arabic, here is a quick reminder of what a passive sentence is. Look at these three sentences in English:

1 A spokesperson for the White House confirmed yesterday that the President was suffering from fatigue.

2 It was confirmed yesterday by a spokesperson for the White House that the President was suffering from fatigue.

3 It was confirmed yesterday that the President was suffering from fatigue.

All of these sentences mean the same. In the first two examples the subject of the verb ("A spokesperson for the White House") is present in the sentence. In sentence 1 the verb is active ("confirmed"); in sentence 2 the verb is passive ("It was confirmed"). The passive puts more emphasis on what is being confirmed rather than who is confirming — which is not so important in this case. In a passive sentence you can still include the subject after the word "by," but it is often omitted altogether, as in sentence 3.

Although you will see the passive from time to time in Arabic, it is not used as much as it is in English. This is partly because the English language is particularly fond of the passive and partly because Arabic has the derived form VII (يَنْفَعِل – *yanfaɛil*), which already has a passive meaning (see Chapter 10). You should be aware of the main features of the passive, but don't worry if you can't remember all the details.

Passive of basic regular verbs

In English we use the verb "to be" + passive participle to form the passive ("it was confirmed," "they are sold," "he has been caught," etc.). Arabic forms the passive by changing the vowels on the tenses.

The past tense of a basic regular verb is vowelized in the passive with a *Damma* followed by a *kasra,* and the present tense with a *Damma* followed by a *fatHa*. This does not vary no matter what the vowels were originally on the active verb:

ذَكَرَ *Dhakara* – mentioned – active past tense →
ذُكِرَ *Dhukira* – was mentioned – passive past tense

شَرِبَ *shariba* – drank – active past tense →
شُرِبَ *shuriba* – was drunk – passive past tense

يَنْطُقُ *yanTuq[u]* – pronounces – active present tense →
يُنْطَقُ *yunTaq[u]* – is pronounced – passive present tense

يَضْرِبُ *yaDrib[u]* – hits – active present tense →
يُضْرَبُ *yuDrab[u]* – is hit – passive present tense

لا يُنْطَق حَرْف القاف في العَرَبِيَّة العامِيَّة المِصْرِيَّة.
The letter *qaaf* is not pronounced in colloquial Egyptian Arabic.

سُرِقَتْ مِني نُقودي!
My money has been stolen from me!

ذُكِرَ هذا الخَبَر عَلَى مَوقِعهم في الإنتَرنَت
This news was mentioned on their website [site on the Internet].

يُشْرَب الشَّرْبات في الأَفْراح.
Sherbet (cordial) is drunk at wedding celebrations.

طُلِبَ مِني أَنْ أَكْتُب جُمَلاً لهذا الكِتاب.
I was asked to write sentences for this book.

Irregular verbs in the passive

Irregular verbs follow the same basic vowelizing as for regular verbs in the passive, with some variations to fit in with the different patterns. Look at this table and the examples that follow:

	Active		**Passive**	
Doubled verbs				
past	عَدَّ	counted	عُدَّ	was counted
present	يَعُدّ	counts	يُعَدّ	is counted
Verbs with hamza				
as 1st root letter:				
past	أَمَرَ	commanded	أُمِرَ	was commanded
present	يَأْمُر	commands	يُؤْمَر	is commanded
as 2nd root letter:				
past	سَأَلَ	asked	سُئِلَ	was asked
present	يَسْأَل	asks	يُسْأَل	is asked
as 3nd root letter:				
past	قَرَأَ	read	قُرِئَ	was read
present	يَقْرَأ	read	يُقْرَأ	is read
Weak verbs				
assimilated:				
past	وَجَدَ	found	وُجِدَ	was found
present	يَجِد	finds	يُوجَد	is found
hollow:				
past	قال	said	قيل	was said
present	يَقول	says	يُقال	is said
defective:				
past	رَمَى	threw	رُمِيَ	was thrown
present	يَرْمي	throws	يُرْمَى	is thrown

Note:

- The middle vowel of the passive reappears on a doubled verb if the second and third root letters are written separately, e.g. عُدِدْت (*udidtu*– I was counted/considered).
- When *hamza* is a root, the letter that carries the hamza can change in the passive as the vowels have changed (see page 34).
- Assimilated verbs have a long *uu* (و) sound at the beginning of the present passive.
- <u>All</u> hollow and weak verbs follow the same pattern in the passive, no matter what group they fall into.

راحة البال لا تقاس بالمال.

Peace of mind is not measured in money. (*Arabic proverb*)

أُعْلِمَ كُلّ مَن يُهِمُّهُ الأَمْر.

Everyone concerned [*lit:* whom the matter concerned] was informed.

قيلَ عَنْكَ كَلام كَثير.

A lot [of talk] was said about you.

أَيْنَ توجَد المعابد الأَثريَّة؟

Where are the historic temples situated [*lit:* found]?

أُمِرَ الجَيش بالهُجوم.

The army was ordered to attack.

Derived forms in the passive

The derived forms are very similar to the basic verb in the passive, with all tenses vowelized initially with a *Damma*. Like the basic verb, the second root letter carries a *kasra* in the past passive and a *fatHa* in the present passive in all the derived forms. Around these vowels, there are some minor variations as shown below:

Derived Form	Past passive		Present passive	
II	كُسِّر	was smashed	يُكَسَّر	is smashed
III	عومِلَ	was treated	يُعامَل	is treated
IV	أُعْلِمَ	was informed	يُعْلَم	is informed
V	تُوُقِّعَ	was expected	يُتَوَقَّع	is expected
VI	تُحودِث	was discussed	يُتَحادَث	is discussed
VII*	—	—	—	—
VIII	أُحْتُرِمَ	was respected	يُحْتَرَم	is respected
X	أُسْتُخْرِجَ	was extracted	يُسْتَخْرَج	is extracted

*Form VII has a passive meaning anyway and is virtually never seen in the passive form.

عُومِلَ المَريض بِعِناية بَعْدَ الجَراحة.

The patient was treated with care after the surgery.

أُعْلِمَ كُلّ مَن يُهِمُّهُ الأَمْر.

Everyone concerned [*lit:* whom the matter concerned] was informed.

يُتَوَقَّع أَنْ يَسْقُط المَطَر بَعْد يَوْمَيْن.

Rain is expected to fall in two days.

يُسْتَخْرَج الذَّهَب مِن المَناجِم.

[The] gold is extracted from [the] mines.

Summary of the passive

- The passive is not as common in Arabic as in English, but you will meet it from time to time.

- The most significant indicator of the passive is the *Damma* (ـُ) at the beginning of both the past and present verbs.

- In the past passive, there is also a *kasra* under the second root letter: فُعِلَ (*fuₑila*).

- In the present passive, there is also a *fatHa* over the second root letter: يُفْعَل (*yufₑal*).

- Irregular verbs and derived forms are variations on the patterns above but need to be referenced individually.

16 Verbal nouns and other verbal constructions

The first fifteen chapters of this book cover the main tenses, variations and derivations of Arabic verbs. This chapter covers verbal nouns and other constructions that are derived from verbs. These follow more or less predictable patterns. Connecting these patterns with a particular type of construction and meaning will help you to further expand your vocabulary and understand the structure of Arabic.

Verbal nouns

In English we make nouns from verbs by adding endings such as "-tion," "-ment," or "-ing" (e.g., "information," "treatment, " "swimming," etc.). Arabic puts the root letters into different patterns to make verbal nouns. These are widely used and you should try to remember the main patterns and uses.

Nouns from basic verbs

Unfortunately as far as the learner is concerned, basic verbs have many different patterns for forming verbal nouns. Here are some of the more common patterns with examples:

Pattern	Example
فَعْل (faɛl)	ضَرْب (Darb – hitting) from يَضْرِب (yaDrib)
فُعول (fuɛuul)	دُخُول (dukhuul – entering) from يَدْخُل (yadkhul)
فَعال (faɛaal)	ذَهاب (dhahaab – going) from يَذْهَب (yadhhab)
فِعالة (fiɛaala)	سِباحة (sibaaHa – swimming) from يَسْبَح (yasbaH)
فَعَل (faɛal)	عَمَل (ɛamal – working) from يَعْمَل (yaɛmal)

However, there are many more patterns for basic verbs, and you will need to look each one up individually in a dictionary. The verbal noun is usually listed together with the verb.

Because of the numerous variations in the way verbal nouns are formed, it is also difficult to generalize about irregular verbs. Some types of irregular verb will behave regularly in some patterns and irregularly in others. Only by looking up and remembering each verbal noun individually will you start to get a feel for how irregular verbs behave and start to take guesses at the likely patterns.

Verbal nouns from derived forms

Verbal nouns from derived forms are much more predictable. Only form III has a widely used alternative. Generally, if you know which derived form a verb is, you will be able to create the verbal noun without reference to a dictionary. The table below shows the verbal noun for the derived forms:

Derived Form	Present verb		Verbal noun	
II	يُكَسِّر	smashes up	تَكْسِير	smashing up
III*	يُعامِل	treats	مُعامَلَة	treatment
IV	يُعْلِم	informs	إعْلام	information
V	يَتَوَقَّع	expects	تَوَقُّع	expectation
VI	يَتَعاوَن	cooperating	تَعاوُن	cooperation
VII	يَنْقَلِب	overturns	إنْقِلاب	overturning
VIII	يَحْتَرِم	respects	إحْتِرام	respect
X	يَسْتَحْسِن	admires	إسْتِحْسان	admiration

*The alternative verbal noun for form III is فِعال as in بِدال (*bidaal* – exchanging).

Uses of verbal nouns

• Generalizations

Verbal nouns are used for generalizing, much as they are in English. Note that you need to include ...َالْ (*al* – the) in Arabic.

السِّبَاحَة مُفِيدة لصِّحّتك.

Swimming is beneficial to your health.

الانْقِلابات تَسْعَى لِتَغْيِير الحُكومات.

Coups attempt to change governments.

الفَنَّانونَ يُحاولونَ أَنْ يُنالوا اسْتِحْسان الجُمْهور.

Artists try to gain the admiration of the public.

• In place of أَنْ (*'an*) + *subjunctive*

Arabic does not have an infinitive like the English "to walk," "to see," etc. Chapter 12 shows how أَنْ (*'an*) + *subjunctive* can be used in Arabic where English would use an infinitive. Another common alternative is to use the verbal noun. Look at these two sentences, which have the same meaning. The first uses أَنْ (*'an*) + *subjunctive* (أَذهَبَ) and the second a verbal noun with *al* (الذَهاب):

أَوَدّ أَنْ أَذهَبَ إلَى السُّوق.

أَوَدّ الذَهاب إلَى السُّوق.

I'd like to go to the market.

It is considered good style to use verbal nouns in this way and is often less clumsy than using a repeating أَنْ. Look at the sentences below and also watch for this usage in authentic Arabic.

زوجي يُريد المُقامرة بمالي أنا!

My husband wants to gamble with <u>my</u> money!

أَرْفُض الدُخول في مُناقشات عَميقة.

I refuse to enter into deep discussions.

• Together with a verb

A verbal noun can be used together with the equivalent verb to add information about the action:

زُرْتُ أُمِّي زِيارة قَصيرة

I visited my mother for a short time [*lit:* a short visit].

طُلِبَتْ مِني طَلَبات كَثيرة كُلُّها صَعْبة.

Many requests have been asked of me, all of them difficult.

تَعاوَنوا مَعَنا تَعاوُناً مُثْمِراً.

They cooperated with us fruitfully [*lit:* a fruitful cooperation].

In addition, many verbal nouns have also acquired a specific meaning in general circulation. For example, the word خِطاب (*khiTaab*) now means "a letter" but is originally the verbal noun from خاطب، يخاطب (*khaaTaba, yukhaaTib*) meaning "to address publicly".

Active and passive participles

An active participle is the equivalent of the English "-ing," as in "I went along the road, <u>whistling</u> a tune."(i.e., I was whistling.) A passive participle is the equivalent of the English "burned" as in "I found the cakes in the oven, <u>burned</u> to a cinder." (i.e., The cakes had been burned.) These can also be used as adjectives to describe something: "a whistling machine," "burnt toast," etc. In Arabic, the active and passive participles are also used to mean "the person/thing that [whistles]" and "the person/thing that is [burned]."

Basic verbs

The active participle is formed by taking the root letters and putting them into the pattern فاعِل (*faaعil*):

كاتِب (*kaatib*) writing/writer

لاعِب (*laaعib*) playing/player

راكِب (*raakib*) riding/rider

The passive participle is formed by putting the root letters into the pattern مَفْعُول (*mafعuul*):

مَسْجُون (*masjuun*) imprisoned/prisoner

مَنْدُوب (*manduub*) delegated/delegate

مَكْسُور (*maksuur*) [thing] broken

Don't forget that the examples above only refer to one masculine person or object. If you want to refer to a female or a group, you will need to add the appropriate ending; for example, كاتبة (*kaatiba*) would be a female writer and لاعبون (*laaɛibuun*) would be a group of players. See Chapters 21 and 22 for more detail on these endings.

Irregular verbs show some variations when put into the patterns for the active and passive participles:

Doubled verbs

active participle	سادّ	blocking
passive participle	مَسْدود	[thing] blocked

Verbs with hamza

as 1st root letter:

active participle	آمِر	commanding/commander
passive participle	مَأْمور	[person] commanded

as 2nd root letter:

active participle	سائِل	asking/asker
passive participle	مَسْؤُول	[person] asked

as 3nd root letter:

active participle	قارِئ	reading/reader
passive participle	مَقْروء	[thing] read

Weak verbs

assimilated (1st root):

active participle	واجِد	finding/finder
passive participle	مَوْجود	[thing] found

hollow (2nd root):

active participle	بائِع	buying/buyer
passive participle	مَبيع/مَقول*	[thing] sold/[thing] said

defective (3rd root):

active participle	قاضٍ**	judging/judge
passive participle	مَقْضِيّ/مَدْعُوّ*	[person] judged/invited

* Alternatives are given for verbs with *waaw* as the weak root letter.

** Pronounced *qaaDin*. A *yaa'* reappears in the definite: القاضي (*al-qaaDii*)

Active and passive participles in the derived forms

Active and passive participles in the derived forms are similar across all the forms and also very similar to each other. All the active and passive participles for derived forms begin with the prefix مـ (*mu*). After that, the vowelizing of the active participle is the same as the present tense, with the *kasra* under the second root letter changing to a *fatHa* for the passive participle. This means that the only thing that separates the active participle مُفَتِّش (*mufattish* – inspector) from the passive particle مُفَتَّش (*mufattash* – inspected) is a single vowel. Because of this, you may find this vowel included for clarity, even on texts that are otherwise not vowelized.

Derived Form	Active participle		Passive participle	
II	مُفَتِّش	inspecting/inspector	مُفَتَّش	inspected
III	مُعاوِن	helping/helper	مُعاوَن	helped
IV	مُرْسِل	sending/sender	مُرْسَل	sent
V	مُتَوَقِّع	expecting	مُتَوَقَّع	expected
VI	مُتَفارِق	dispersing	مُتَفارَق	dispersed
VII	مُنْصَرِف	departing	مُنْصَرَف	departed
VIII	مُحْتَرِم	respecting	مُحْتَرَم	respected
X	مُسْتَعْمِل	utilizing	مُسْتَعْمَل	utilized

Here are some example sentences showing active and passive participles in context:

الشيكات المُرْسِلة بالبَريد تَأَخَّرَتْ في الوُصول.

The checks that were mailed were late in arriving.

كُلّ مُسْتَعْمِل لِهذا النَفَق يُخْتَصِر مِن رِحْلتِهِ ساعتَين.

Every user of this tunnel cuts two hours from his journey.

تَجَوَّلَت المُفَتِّشات بَينَ الفصول في المَدْرَسة.

The [female] inspectors alternated between cl…

اِشْتَرَيْنا كُلَّ الخُبْز المَوْجود في المَخْبَز.

We bought all the bread found in the bakery.

مُصمِّمو المَوقِع كانوا مِن المُحْتَرِفين.

The website designers were professionals.

Nouns of place and instrument

Other nouns that are derived from verbs are *nouns of place* and *nouns of instrument*.

Nouns of place describe the place where an action happens. They are formed by putting the root letters of a verb into the pattern مَفْعَل (*mafₑal*), مَفْعِل (*mafₑil*), or مَفْعَلة (*mafₑala*):

مَدْرَسة (*madrasa* – school ["place of study"]) from درس (to study)

مَكْتَب (*maktab* – desk/office ["place of writing"]) from كتب (to write)

مَصْنَع(*maSnaₑ* – factory ["place of manufacture"]) from صنع (to manufacture)

مَجْلِس (*majlis* – council ["place of sitting"]) from جلس (to sit)

Nouns of instrument describe the implement used to perform an action. They are formed by putting the root letters of a verb into the pattern مِفْعَل (*mifₑal*), مِفْعال (*mifₑaal*), or مِفْعَلة (*mifₑala*):

مِفْتاح (*miftaH* – key ["instrument of opening"]) from فتح (to open)

مِكْنَسة(*miknasa* – broom ["instrument of sweeping"]) from كنس (to sweep)

مِقَصّ (*miqaSS* – scissors ["instrument of cutting"]) from قصّ (to cut)

مِنْشار (*minshaar* – saw ["instrument of sawing"]) from نشر (to saw)

Summary of verbal nouns and other verbal constructions

- There are a number of nouns and participles that can be formed from verbs. The most important of these are verbal nouns, active and passive participles, nouns of place, and nouns of instrument. Familiarizing yourself with the patterns connected to each of these will help you expand your vocabulary.

- Verbal nouns are formed from the root letters of a verb using a variety of patterns. These patterns are more predictable in the derived forms than in the basic form. Verbal nouns are mainly used for generalizations and in sentences where English would use an infinitive ("to walk"/"to see," etc.)

- Active participles follow the pattern فاعِل (*faaɛil*) in the basic verb. In the derived forms they all start with the sound مـ (*mu*) and have a *kasra* as the final vowel. They are the rough equivalent of the English "-ing," but can also be used to describe the person/thing carrying out an action.

- Passive participles follow the pattern مَفْعُول (*mafɛuul*) in the basic verb. In the derived forms they are the same as the active participle, except that they have *fatHa* as the final vowel. They are the equivalent of the English past participle (burned/drunk, etc.), but can also be used to describe the person/thing that is the object of an action.

- There are also patterns that are used to describe the place or instrument of an action. Nouns of place start with مـ (*ma*) and nouns of instrument with مـ (*mi*). The vowels after this vary and each word should be learned individually.

17 Verbs in the dual

Arabic distinguishes between two things or people (the *dual*) and more than two (the *plural*). Chapter 28 gives a more detailed overview of the dual, but this chapter specifically looks at the dual verb endings.

The dual verb endings have been deliberately separated so that you can tackle them only when you are confident with other aspects and types of the verb.

There are three different dual endings for the following:

أَنْتُمَا (*'antumaa*: you two – both masculine and feminine)

هُمَا (*humaa*: they two – masculine*)

هُمَا (*humaa*: they two – feminine*)

*Note that although the word for the dual "they" is هُمَا (*humaa*) for both masculine and feminine, the verb endings are different.

Here are the dual endings for the verb كَتَبَ/يَكْتُب (to write):

	Past	**Present**	**Subjunctive***	**Jussive***
أَنْتُمَا	كَتَبْتُمَا (*katabtumaa*)	تَكْتُبَانِ (*taktubaani*)	تَكْتُبَا (*taktubaa*)	تَكْتُبَا (*taktubaa*)
هُمَا (*masc.*)	كَتَبَا (*katabaa*)	يَكْتُبَانِ (*yaktubaani*)	يَكْتُبَا (*yaktubaa*)	يَكْتُبَا (*yaktubaa*)
هُمَا (*fem.*)	كَتَبَتَا (*katabataa*)	تَكْتُبَانِ (*taktubaani*)	تَكْتُبَا (*taktubaa*)	تَكْتُبَا (*taktubaa*)

* Note that the dual loses the final *nuun* in the subjunctive and jussive as the masculine plurals do.

Irregular verbs will follow the same rules in the dual as those for other parts of the verb. Also note that, like the plural, a verb will only be dual if it comes <u>after</u> the subject; otherwise it will be singular (see page 63 for more details.)

العائِلتان هـاجَرَتا إلى كَنَدا بَعْدَ الحَرْب.

The two families emigrated to Canada after the war.

هذان الفيلان يَشْتركان في عُروض السيرْك.

These two elephants take part in the circus parades.

تُريد ابْنَتايَ أَنْ تَتَفَوَّقا في امْتِحان اللُّغة الفَرَنْسِيَّة.

My two daughters want to succeed in the French language examination.

18 Verbs with four root letters (quadriliterals)

Most Arabic verbs have three root letters, but there are a few that have four. These verbs are called *quadriliteral* (رُباعي). A few of these verbs are reasonably common and you will need to recognize them.

Basic quadriliteral verb

A basic quadriliteral verb is vowelized very similarly to form II of a triliteral verb (verb with three root letters.) The past tense is vowelized with all *fatHas* and the present with *Damma/fatHa/kasra*:

Past tense: دَحْرَجَ (*daHraja*) – rolled

Present tense: يُدَحْرِج (*yudaHrij*) – rolls

The active and passive participles are also very similar to form II:

Active participle: مُدَحْرِج (*mudaHrij*) – rolling

Passive participle: مُدَحْرَج (*mudaHraj*) – (been) rolled

The most common verbal noun pattern from a basic quadriliteral verb is دَحْرَجة (*daHraja*), although some minor variations exist.

Many verbs with four root letters are in fact created by repeating the same sequence of two letters. This is often used for *onomatopoeic* verbs (verbs that sound similar to their meaning:)

يُثَرْثِر (*yutharthir*) – to chatter

يُغَرْغِر (*yugharghir*) – to gargle

يُتَمْتِم (*yutamtim*) – to mutter

يُدَنْدِن (*yudandin*) – to hum

Derived forms of quadriliteral verbs

In theory, there are three derived forms for quadriliteral verbs. In practice, form III is virtually extinct and there are no more than a handful of verbs in the other two forms in common circulation. However, for the sake of these verbs, here are the past and present tenses for forms II and IV of quadriliteral verbs:

Form II

Past tense: تَفَلْسَفَ (*tafalsafa*) – philosophized
Present tense: يَتَفَلْسَف (*yatafalsaf*) – philosophizes

Form IV

Past tense: إقْشَعَرَّ (*iqshaɛarra*) – shuddered/quaked
Present tense: يَقْشَعِرّ (*yaqshaɛirr*) – shudders/quakes

Here are some examples of quadriliteral verbs in context:

أُدَنْدِن تَحْتَ الدُش.
I hum in [*lit:* under] the shower.

أَنْتِ تُثَرْثِرِينَ عَلَى التَليفون مُنْذُ الصَباح.
You [*fem.*] have been chattering on the telephone since the morning.

تَسَلْسَلَتْ أَحْداث الفيلْم بِإِيقاع سَريع.
The events of the film followed one another at a fast pace.

الخَشَب الرَطِب يُطَقْطِق في المَدْفَأَة.
Damp wood crackles in the fireplace.

19 Some unusual common verbs

A few verbs have particular oddities, usually because of multiple combinations of irregular features. The most important of these are listed below. Since they are some of the most common verbs in the Arabic language, you will need to try and memorize them individually.

جاء/يجيء (to come)

This verb represents the most common group of very irregular verbs: hollow verbs that also have *hamza* as the last root letter. Both the rules applying to hollow verbs and the rules for the spelling of *hamza* apply to these verbs, causing multiple changes.

singular	Past		Present		Subjunctive		Jussive	
أنا	جِئْتُ	(ji'tu)	أَجِيءُ ('ajii'[u])		أَجِيءَ ('ajii'[a])		أَجِئْ	(aji')
أَنْتَ	جِئْتَ	(ji'ta)	تَجِيءُ (tajii'[u])		تَجِيءَ (tajii'[a])		تَجِئْ	(taji')
أَنْتِ	جِئْتِ	(ji'ti)	تَجِيئِينَ (tajii'iina)		تَجِيئِي (tajii'ii)		تَجِيئِي	(tajii'ii)
هُوَ	جاءَ	(jaa'a)	يَجِيءُ (yajii'[u])		يَجِيءَ (yajii'[a])		يَجِئْ	(yaji')
هِيَ	جاءَتْ	(jaa'at)	تَجِيءُ (tajii'[u])		تَجِيءَ (tajii'[a])		تَجِئْ	(taji')
plural								
نَحْنُ	جِئْنا	(ji'naa)	نَجِيءُ (najii'[u])		نَجِيءَ (najii'[a])		نَجِئْ	(naji')
أَنْتُمْ	جِئْتُمْ	(ji'tum)	تَجِيئُونَ (tajii'uuna)		تَجِيئُوا (tajii'uu)		تَجِيئُوا	(tajii'uu)
أَنْتُنَّ	جِئْتُنَّ	(ji'tunna)	تَجِئْنَ (taji'na)		تَجِئْنَ (taji'na)		تَجِئْنَ	(taji'na)
هُم	جاءوا	(jaa'uu)	يَجِيئُونَ (yajii'uuna)		يَجِيئُوا (yajii'uu)		يَجِيئُوا	(yajii'uu)
هُنَّ	جِئْنَ	(ji'na)	يَجِئْنَ (yaji'na)		يَجِئْنَ (yaji'na)		يَجِئْنَ	(yaji'na)

جاءوا إلى بَيتي بَعْدَ خُروجي.

They came to my house after I had left [*lit*: after my leaving].

لَمْ أَجِئْ لأَنِّي مَريض.

I didn't come because I'm sick.

رأى/يرى (to see)

This verb has the root letters ر (*raa'*) + ء (*hamza*) + ي (*yaa'*). It acts relatively normally in the past, but drops the *hamza* altogether in the present. Pay particular attention to the *jussive*. The *yaa'* also gets dropped, which makes for a very short verb!

singular	**Past**		**Present**		**Subjunctive**		**Jussive**	
أنا	رَأَيْتُ	(ra'aytu)	أَرَى	('araa)	أَرَى	('araa)	أَرَ	('ara)
أَنْتَ	رَأَيْتَ	(ra'ayta)	تَرَى	(taraa)	تَرَى	(taraa)	تَرَ	(tara)
أَنْتِ	رَأَيْتِ	(ra'ayti)	تَرَيْنَ	(tarayna)	تَرَيْ	(taray)	تَرَيْ	(taray)
هُوَ	رَأَى	(ra'aa)	يَرَى	(yaraa)	يَرَى	(yaraa)	يَرَ	(yara)
هِيَ	رَأَتْ	(ra'at)	تَرَى	(taraa)	تَرَى	(taraa)	تَرَ	(tara)
plural								
نَحْنُ	رَأَيْنا	(ra'aynaa)	نَرَى	(naraa)	نَرَى	(naraa)	نَرَ	(nara)
أَنْتُمْ	رَأَيْتُمْ	(ra'aytum)	تَرَوْنَ	(tarawna)	تَرَوْا	(taraw)	تَرَوْا	(taraw)
أَنْتُنَّ	رَأَيْتُنَّ	(ra'aytunna)	تَرَيْنَ	(tarayna)	تَرَيْنَ	(tarayna)	تَرَيْنَ	(tarayna)
هُم	رأَوْا	(ra'aw)	يَرَوْنَ	(yarawna)	يَرَوْا	(yaraw)	يَرَوْا	(yaraw)
هُنَّ	رَأَيْنَ	(ra'ayna)	يَرَيْنَ	(yarayna)	يَرَيْنَ	(yarayna)	يَرَيْنَ	(yarayna)

هَلْ رَأَيْتَ آلة الطِّباعة الجَديدة في المَعْرَض؟

Did you see the new printing machine at the exhibition?

أُريد أَنْ أَرى أُمّي.

I want to see my mother.

لَمْ يَرَ الزبون المَصْنَع الجَديد أمْس.

The client didn't see the new factory yesterday.

لَيْسَ (not to be)

Arabic does not have a verb "to be" (is/are/am, etc.) in simple positive sentences (see Chapter 23 for more details.) However, it does have a verb "not to be." The sentence:

هاني طَبيب. Haanii (is) a doctor.

can be made negative by adding لَيْسَ or لَيْسَ...بِـ:

لَيْسَ هاني طَبيبًا*. Haanii isn't a doctor.

لَيْسَ هاني بِطَبيب. Haanii isn't a doctor.

* طبيب now has the accusative ending طبيبًا (*Tabiiban*) – see Appendix (ii).

لَيْسَ is unusual because it looks like a past verb, but always has a present meaning ("Haani <u>wasn't</u> a doctor" would be لَمْ يَكُنْ هاني طبيباً).
However, it does change according to the subject:

لَسْتُ I'm not

لَسْتَ/لَسْتِ/لَسْتُمْ you're not (*masc./fem./pl.*)

لَيْسَ he's not

لَيْسَتْ she's not

لَسْنا we're not

لَيْسوا/لَسْنَ they're not (*masc./fem.*)

المُوَظَّفون لَيْسوا في المَكْتَب قَبْلَ الساعة التاسِعة.

The employees are not in the office before nine o'clock.

لَسْتُ بِمُدَرِّس.

I'm not a teacher.

Part Two:
Arabic Essentials of Grammar

20 The article and personal pronouns

الـ al (definite article)

Arabic does not have an equivalent of the English "a/an" (indefinite article) as in "a book/an apple." The word is simply written by itself:

كِتاب (*kitaab*) a book

بِنْت (*bint*) a girl

مُدَرِّس (*mudarris*) a teacher

However, there is an equivalent of "the" (*definite article*): الـ (*al*). This is joined to the beginning of the word, rather than written separately.

اَلْكِتاب (*al-kitaab*) the book

اَلْبِنْت (*al-bint*) the girl

اَلْمُدَرِّس (*al-mudarris*) the teacher

The *fatHa* (*a*) is dropped from *al* when the previous word ends in a vowel:

وَجَدَ الْكِتاب. (*wajada l-kitaab*) He found the book.

هذِهِ الْبِنْت (*haadhihi l-bint*) this girl

Sometimes, the *lam* (ل) of the word الـ is pronounced the same as the first letter of the word that follows:

اَلسَّيّارة (*as-sayyara*) the car

اَلرَّجُل (*ar-rajul*) the man

اَلتُّفّاحة (*at-tuffaHa*) the apple

Notice how the first letter of the word now has a *shadda* (ـّ) over it to show that it is doubled. There are fourteen letters in Arabic that cause *al* to change. These letters are called "sun letters" (الحُروف الشَّمْسِيّة), and you can find a full list of them in Appendix (i). Pronouncing these correctly is something that will take experience and time but will eventually become automatic.

Personal pronouns

Personal pronouns are the equivalent of the English "I/we/you/she/he," etc. These are:

singular

أنَا (*'ana*) I

أنْتَ (*'anta*) you [*masculine*]

أنْتِ (*'anti*) you [*feminine*]

هُوَ (*huwa*) he/it

هِيَ (*hiya*) she/it

plural

نَحْنُ (*naHnu*) we

أنْتُمْ (*'antum*) you [*pl. masculine*]

أنْتُنَّ (*'antunna*) you [*pl. feminine*]

هُمْ (*hum*) they [*masculine*]

هُنَّ (*hunna*) they [*feminine*]

(The next chapter explains more about feminine and masculine.)

Note that Arabic also has different pronouns for "you" and "they" when talking about two people (*the dual*). See Chapter 28 for details on these.

21 Genders

Arabic, like many other languages, makes a difference between male and female nouns (people, objects, ideas, etc.) It has two *genders*: *masculine* (male) and *feminine* (female). The gender of a noun will affect other words in a sentence, such as verbs, adjectives, etc., so you need to be confident in this aspect of the grammar.

Luckily, unlike many other languages, it is usually easy to tell the difference between masculine and feminine nouns in Arabic. There are only a few exceptions to the general rules.

There are two main categories of feminine words:

Words that refer to females — e.g.,:

بِنْت (*bint*) girl

أُمّ (*'umm*) mother

لَيْلَى (*layla*) Layla (or any other girl's name)

Note that most countries are also regarded as feminine.

Words that end in ة (*taa' marbuuTa*):

There is a special feminine ending that is a cross between ت (*taa'*) and ه (*ha'*): ة. This is called *taa' marbuuTa*. The vowel before a *taa' marbuuTa* is always a *fatHa*. Words that end with *taa' marbuuTa* are almost always feminine.

مَدِينَة (*madiina*) city

مَكْتَبَة (*maktaba*) bookstore

فِكْرة (*fikra*) idea

Usually, the *taa' marbuuTa* is not pronounced — only the *fatHa* that comes before it.

There are many feminine words that fit into both of the categories above, ending in *taa' marbuuTa* <u>and</u> referring to female people:

زَوْجة (*zawja*) wife

مُمَرِّضة (*mumariDDa*) [female] nurse

خالة (*khaala*) [maternal] aunt

There are also a few feminine words that do not fit into either category. Most of these are parts of the body or are connected with the natural world. Here are some examples of these.

شَمْس (*shams*) sun

يَد (*yad*) hand

أَرْض ('*arD*) earth

رِجْل (*rijl*) foot

In general, however, you can assume a word is masculine unless it refers to a female or ends in *taa' marbuuTa*.

22 Sentences without verbs

In Arabic, the verb "to be" (e.g., I <u>am</u>, you <u>are</u>, he <u>is</u>, etc.) is omitted in simple present sentences. This means that in Arabic, unlike in English, you can have a sentence with no verb at all:

أَحْمَد مُدَرِّس. Ahmed (is a) teacher.

أَنا مَشْغول اليَوم. I (am) busy today.

أُمّي في الحَمام. My mother (is) in the bathroom.

الشُّبّاك مكْسور. The window (is) broken.

These types of sentences are called "nominal sentences."

Demonstrative pronouns

You will often find nominal sentences using the Arabic equivalents of "this" and "that" (*demonstrative pronouns*):

هذا (*haadhaa*) this (masculine singular)

هذِه (*haadhihi*) this (feminine singular)

هَؤُلاءِ (*haa'ulaa'i*) these (plural*)

ذلِكَ (*dhaalika*) that (masculine singular)

تِلْكَ (*tilka*) that (feminine singular)

أُولئِكَ (*'ulaa'ika*) those (plural*)

*The plurals are only used for people. For nonhuman plurals, use the feminine singular — see Chapter 23.

هذا كِتاب. This (is a) book.

هذِهِ أُخْتي. This (is) my sister.

تِلكَ أُمّي. That (is) my mother.

هؤُلاءِ مُوَظَّفون في شَرِكتي. These (are) employees in my company.

Be careful to distinguish between the following:

هذا كِتاب. (*haadhaa kitaab*) This (is) a book.

هذا الكِتاب... (*haadhaa l-kitaab*) This book...

The first is a sentence, the second is not. You need to add the appropriate pronoun, in this case هو (*huwa*), if you want to say the sentence "This is the book.":

هذا هُوَ الكِتاب. (*haadhaa huwa l-kitaab*) This (is) the book.

هذِهِ هِيَ المُشْكِلة. (*haadhihi hiya l-mushkila*) This (is) the problem.

You should include the appropriate form of the verb يَكون (*yakuun*) if a sentence requires you to use the *subjunctive, jussive,* or *imperative* (see Chapters 12 and 13 for when these are used):

أحْمَد يُريد أنْ يكون مُدَرِّساً. Ahmed wants to be a teacher.

كُنْ لَطيفاً مَعَ أُخْتِكَ. Be gentle with your sister.

لا تكونوا كَسالَى. Don't be [*plural*] lazy.

If you want to make a nominal sentence negative, you need to use the special verb لَيْسَ (see page 101).

23 Describing things

Adjectives are the words you use to describe something, such as the English "happy," "heavy," "red," "busy," etc. In English, adjectives come <u>before</u> the person or thing described (the *noun*) and do not change depending on whether the noun is singular or plural, etc.:

a happy baby
happy babies

a red light
red lights

In Arabic, adjectives come <u>after</u> the noun and change depending on whether the noun is singular or plural, masculine or feminine.

Masculine and feminine adjectives

If the noun described is feminine, then the adjective is also feminine. (If you are unsure about masculine and feminine nouns, then review Chapter 21.) This usually means adding the feminine ending ة (*taa' marbuuTa*) to the adjective:

مُدَرِّس مَشْغول   (a) busy teacher [*masculine*]

مُدَرِّسة مَشْغولة   (a) busy teacher [*feminine*]

كِتاب ثَقيل   (a) heavy book [*masculine*]

حَقيبة ثَقيلة   (a) heavy bag [*feminine*]

All of the above examples are *indefinite* ("a busy teacher"). If you want to make them *definite* (<u>the</u> busy teacher) you have to add الـ (*al*) to both the noun and the adjective:

المُدَرِّس المَشْغُول   the busy teacher

الكِتاب الثَقيل   the heavy book

الحَقيبة الثَقيلة   the heavy bag

There are a few adjectives to which you cannot add *taa' marbuuTa* to make the feminine. They have different feminine forms. The most important of these are the adjectives describing the primary colors:

Color	Masculine	Feminine
red	أَحْمَر ('aHmar)	حَمْراء (Hamraa')
blue	أَزْرَق ('azraq)	زَرْقاء (zarqaa')
yellow	أَصْفَر ('aSfar)	صَفْراء (Safraa')
black	أَسْوَد ('aswad)	سَوْداء (sawdaa')
white	أَبْيَض ('abyaD)	بَيْضاء (bayDaa')
green	أَخْضَر ('akhDar)	خَضْراء (khaDraa')

Adjectives with plurals

Adjectives also have a different plural form, but it is very important to remember that these will only be used with people. Nonhumans (things, ideas, etc.) use <u>feminine singular</u> adjectives.

Many adjectives begin with مُ (*mu*) and are participles of the derived forms of the verb (see Chapter 16). These can be made plural by adding ـُونَ (*uuna*) for males and ـات (*aat*) for females, but others have their own particular plurals. It is best to check in a dictionary, which will give the plural after the adjective. Here are some examples of adjectives used with humans and nonhuman plurals so that you can compare them. For a more complete overview of the plural in general, see Chapter 25.

ظُروف مُناسَبة suitable circumstances

مُوَظَّفونَ مُناسَبونَ suitable [male] employees

مُوَظَّفات مُناسَبات suitable [female] employees

كُتُب جَديدة new books

مُدَرِّسونَ جُدُد new [male] teachers

Comparatives

If you want to compare two things, you will need to use the comparative form of the adjective. The rules for forming the comparative are similar to English.

Comparatives with simple adjectives

In English, we put "-er" on the end of short words to make a comparative: "longer/shorter/richer/poorer," etc. In Arabic, the root letters of a simple adjective are put into the pattern أَفْعَل (*'afal*) to make a comparative:

كَبير (*kabiir*) big → أَكْبَر (*'akbar*) bigger

قَصير (*qaSiir*) short → أَقْصَر (*'aqSar*) shorter

لَطيف (*laTiif*) gentle → أَلْطَف (*'alTaf*) gentler

If an adjective has a doubled root, they are written together. If it ends in a و (*waaw*) or a ي (*yaa'*), this becomes an *'alif maqSuura* (*yaa'* with no dots pronounced *aa*):

جَديد (*jadiid*) new → أَجَدّ (*'ajadd*) newer

ذَكِيّ (*dhakiiy*) clever → أَذْكَى (*'adhkaa*) cleverer

The equivalent of the English "than," as in "better than," is the Arabic word مِنْ (*min*). You will most often find the comparative used in this way. It does <u>not</u> change depending on whether the word it is describing is masculine or feminine:

أَخي أَقْصَر مِنْ أُخْتي.   My brother is shorter than my sister.

القاهِرة أكْبَر مِنْ الخَرْطوم.   Cairo is bigger than Khartoum.

If you add الـ (*al*) to a comparative, the meaning becomes *superlative* the equivalent of the English "-est", as in "bigg<u>est</u>, short<u>est</u>," etc.:

أَخي هُوَ الأَقْصَر في العائِلة.   My brother [he] is the shortest in the family.

البريد الإلِكتروني هُوَ الأَسْرَع.   Electronic mail [it] is the fastest.

Comparatives with longer adjectives

In English, when we have a long adjective we want to make comparative, we use the word "more" (or "less"), rather than putting "-er" on the end: "<u>more</u> comfortable/<u>more</u> suitable/<u>less</u> adaptable."

Arabic is similar. The word أكْثَر (*'akthar* – "more") or أقَلّ (*'aqall* – "less") is added in front of the <u>noun</u> to make the comparative:

أكْثَر مُلائمة   more suitable

أكْثَر اِحْتِراماً   more respected

أقَلّ اِسْتِعْمالاً   less utilized

Note: The nouns are now in the accusative case (*mulaa'amatan*, etc.) — see Appendix (ii).

24 Describing position (prepositions of place)

The following words are commonly used to describe the position of something, and are also sometimes known as *prepositions of place*.

عَلَى (ع*alaa*) on

في (*fii*) in

إلَى ('*ilaa*) to(ward)

فَوْقَ (*fawqa*) above

تَحْتَ (*taHta*) under

أَمامَ ('*amaama*) in front of

وَراءَ (*waraa'a*) behind

بَيْنَ (*bayna*) between

حَوْلَ (*Hawla*) around

مَعَ (*ma*ع*a*) with

بِجانِب (*bijaanib*) next to

عِنْدَ (ع*inda*) with (someone), "chez"

Examples:

المَلَفّ تَحْتَ المَكْتَب.
The file is under the desk.

المُدير العامّ عِنْدَ عَميل اليَوْم.
The general manager is with a client today.

ذَهَبْتُ إلَى البَنْك أَمْس.
I went to the bank yesterday.

وَجَدْتُ صَديقي وَراءَ البَيْت في الحَديقة.
I found my friend behind the house in the garden.

هَلْ رَأَيْتَ نَظّارتي عَلَى البيانو؟
Did you see my glasses on the piano?

25 Plurals

In English, plurals are words referring to <u>more than one</u> thing and are generally formed by adding the letter -*s*: book<u>s</u>, idea<u>s</u>, letter<u>s</u>, etc. There are some words to which you have to add -*es* – box<u>es</u>, church<u>es</u> – and a few isolated irregularities, such as "man" becoming "men."

In Arabic, plurals refer to <u>more than two</u> things. The dual form is used for two (see Chapter 28.) In addition, most plurals are more like the English "man/men" example than a case of simply adding letters on the end of a word.

Plurals are one of the few genuinely complicated areas of basic Arabic grammar. This chapter will give you the essentials, but be prepared to learn each plural individually with the singular.

Forming plurals

Learning how to form the plural for Arabic words is a long and sometimes frustrating business. However, if you persevere, you will eventually learn most of the common plurals and acquire an instinct for the others.

Sound plurals

All plurals are classified as either *sound* or *broken*. Sound plurals are the simplest to learn but have limitations in how widely they are used. There are two sound plurals:

Masculine: formed by adding وﻥَ- (-*uuna**) on the end of the singular and used mainly (but not exclusively) for male professions:

مُدَرِّس (*mudarris*) teacher → مُدَرِّسُونَ (*mudarrisuuna*) teachers

نَجّار (*najjaar*) carpenter → نَجّارونَ (*najjaaruuna*) carpenters

* Changes to ﻴﻦِ- (-*iina*) in the accusative and genitive case — see Appendix (ii).

Feminine: formed by adding ـَات (*-aat*) on the end of the singular. If the word ends in a *taa' marbuuTa* (ة), this must be removed first. Like its masculine equivalent, the sound feminine plural is used for professions but is also used for a number of other words, especially verbal nouns from the derived forms (see Chapter 16.)

مُدَرِّسة (*mudarrisa*) teacher [*fem.*] → مُدَرِّسات (*mudarrisaat*) teachers

اِجْتِماع (*ijtimaaع*) meeting → اِجْتِماعَات (*ijtimaaعaat*) meetings

اِصْلاح (*iSlaaH*) reform → اِصْلاحات (*iSlaaHaat*) reforms

Broken plurals

The majority of plurals are broken plurals, so called because the singular is broken apart and different long and short vowels are arranged around the root letters. Look at this example of how the plural of the word وَلَد (*walad* – boy) is formed:

singular:

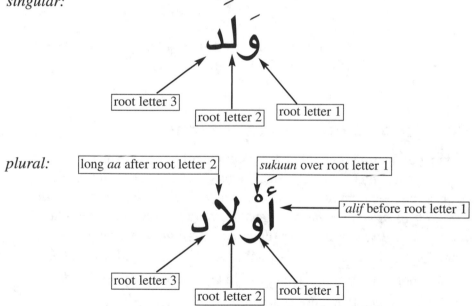

plural:

This plural pattern is the أَفْعَال (*'afaal*) pattern, with the letters *faa'* (ف), *ع ayn* (ع), and *lam* (ل) representing the three root letters. There are many different plural patterns, but some are more common than others. It does not matter how the singular is vowelized, the plural pattern will always be the same, except that you have to know which to use!

Here are the eight of the most common patterns with examples.

Pattern	Example plural	Singular of...
أَفْعال (*'afɛaal*)	أَقْلام (*'aqlaam*)	قَلَم (*qalam:* pen)
فُعول (*fuɛuul*)	بُيوت (*buyuut*)	بَيْت (*bayt:* house)
فِعال (*fiɛaal*)	كِلاب (*kilaab*)	كَلْب (*kalb:* dog)
فُعُل (*fuɛul*)	كُتُب (*kutub*)	كِتاب (*kitaab:* book)
فُعَل (*fuɛal*)	دُوَل (*duwal*)	دَوْلة (*dawla:* country)
أَفْعُل (*'afɛul*)	أَشْهُر (*'ashhur*)	شَهْر (*shahr:* month)
فُعَلاء (*fuɛalaa'*)	وُزَراء (*wuzaraa'*)	وَزير (*waziir:* minister)
أَفْعِلاء (*'afɛilaa'*)	أَصْدِقاء (*'aSdiqaa'*)	صَديق (*Sadiiq:* friend)

You will have to look in a dictionary to find which pattern to use for an individual word. The plural will be given after the singular.

Human and nonhuman plurals

Arabic grammar has two different categories of plural: human (e.g. "men," "nurses," etc.) and nonhuman (e.g., "books," "negotiations," etc.). This distinction is <u>very</u> important to remember. *The masculine and feminine plural forms of verbs, adjectives, etc. are only used with human plural nouns. Nonhuman plurals are regarded as feminine singular.* So, for example, the plural كُتُب (*kutub* – books) would be referred to as هِيَ (*hiya* – she) and <u>not</u> هُم (*hum* – they), and would be described as جَديدة (*jadiida* – new [*fem. singular*]) and <u>not</u> جُدُد (*judud* – new [*masc. plural*]):

هذِهِ هِيَ الكُتُب الجَديدة. These are the new books.

اِنْتَهَت المُناقَشات أَمْس. The discussions ended (*intahat* – fem. sing.) yesterday.

You need to etch this concept into your brain. Look back at the verb chapters and remind yourself of the feminine singular verbs. You could practice by forming a few sentences using nonhuman plurals.

26 Describing possession

إضافة ('iDaafa)

In English, we have two main ways of describing possession – using the word "of," or the possessive " -'s ":

the client's office

the office of the client

The most common way of describing possession in Arabic is closer to the second example above, in that the word for "office" would come first followed by the word for "client." The difference is that the two words are put directly together (the meaning "of" is understood) and only the last word can have the article الـ (al):

مكْتَب العَميل the office of the client

بَيْت المُدَرِّس the teacher's house

وَزير الاقْتِصـاد the minister of the economy

This structure, where two (or more) nouns are put back to back, is known as إضافة ('iDaafa), which literally means "addition." Nothing can come between two words in an 'iDaafa. So if you want to add an adjective, it must come right at the end and will have the article الـ (al):

مكْتَب العَميل المُرْتَفِع the elevated office of the client

بَيْت المُدَرِّس الفَخْم the teacher's luxurious house

وَزير الاقْتِصـاد المِصْرِيّ the Egyptian minister of the economy

Watch out for the *sound masculine plural* and the *dual* when they are the first noun in an 'iDaafa. They lose the final *nuun* (ن):

مُدَرِّسون teachers ← مُدَرِّسُو* المَدْرسة the teachers of the school

مُدَرِّسانِ two teachers ← مُدَرِّسا** المَدْرسة the two teachers of the school

* Changes to ـي (-ii) in the accusative and genitive case – see Appendix (ii).

** Changes to ـَي (-ay) in the accusative and genitive case – see Appendix (ii).

The *taa' marbuuTa* on the end of most feminine nouns is pronounced when the word is the first in the *'iDaafa*:

مَدينة لُنْدُن (*madiinat lundun*) the city of London

Possessive (attached) pronouns

Possessive pronouns are the equivalent of the English "my," "his," "ours," etc. In Arabic they are <u>joined to the end</u> of the word and are also known as *attached pronouns*:

مَكْتَبِنا (*maktabnaa*) our office

بَيْتِي (*baytii*) my house

Here is a table of the possessive pronouns with the example showing the ending on the word بَيت (*bayt* – house):

		Possessive ending	Example
أَنا	I	ـِي (ii)**	بَيْتِي (baytii)
أَنْتَ	you (masc.)	كَ (ka)	بَيْتُكَ (bayt[u*]ka)
أَنْتِ	you (fem.)	كِ (ki)	بَيْتُكِ (bayt[u]ki)
هُوَ	he/it	ـهُ (hu)	بَيْتُهُ (bayt[u]hu)
هِيَ	she/it	ـهَا (haa)	بَيْتُهَا (bayt[u]haa)
نَحْنُ	we	ـنَا (naa)	بَيْتُنَا (bayt[u]naa)
أَنْتُمْ	you (masc. pl.)	كُمْ (kum)	بَيْتُكُمْ (bayt[u]kum)
أَنْتُنَّ	you (fem. pl.)	كُنَّ (kunna)	بَيْتُكُنَّ (bayt[u]kunna)
هُمْ	they (masc. pl.)	ـهُمْ (hum)	بَيْتُهُمْ (bayt[u]hum)
هُنَّ	they (fem. pl.)	ـهُنَّ (hunna)	بَيْتُهُنَّ (bayt[u]hunna)

Notes to the table:

* The additional *Damma* (ُ [u]) is the nominative case ending, which can change to *fatHa* or *kasra* – see Appendix (ii). Note that the endings هُ (*hu*) and هُمْ (*hum*) become هِ (*hi*) and هِم (*him*) if this additional vowel is a *kasra*: بَيْتِهِ (*baytihi*), بَيْتِهِمْ (*baytihim*).

** The *ii* ending changes to *ya* if the word finishes in a long vowel: مُحامِيَّ (*muHaamiiya* – my attorney).

Attached pronouns can also be used with verbs, prepositions, and words such as أَنَّ (*'anna* – that).

Attached pronouns with verbs

You can add the pronouns in the table opposite to verbs, except that the ending ي (*ii*) changes to نِ (*nii*). The other endings are the same:

أَخَذْتُها مَعي.   I took her with me.

باعوه أَمْس.   They sold it yesterday.

تَزورنا كُلّ أُسْبوع.   She visits us every week.

Attached pronouns with prepositions and أَنَّ

The attached pronouns can also be put on prepositions (see Chapter 24 for examples of prepositions) and words such as أَنَّ.

Note that the *nuun* of the preposition مِن (*min* – from) is doubled when *ii* is added:

أَخَذَتْ أُمّي فُلوسي مِنّي.   My mother took my money from me.

The word أَنَّ is pronounced *'anna* before an attached pronoun (or noun), except for أَنِّي (*'annii* – "that I"):

ذَكَرَتْ أَنَّها تَحْتاج إلَيْها.   She mentioned that she needed it.

شَكَوْتُ أَنِّي مُفْلِس.   I complained that I was broke.

27 Questions and relative clauses

Questions

Questions are straightforward in Arabic. There is no special form of the verb used with questions. Simple questions can be formed by adding a question mark to the end of a sentence or by putting the word هَلْ (*hal*), or less commonly أ ('*a*), in front of it:

هذا كِتاب. This is a book.

هَلْ هذا كِتاب؟/ أهذا كِتاب؟ Is this a book?

Other questions are formed by using the appropriate question word:

أَيْنَ البَنْك؟ Where is the bank?   مَتَى نَذْهَب؟ When are we going?

ماذا* تَفْعَل؟ What are you doing?   مَنْ وَجَدَ المِفْتاح؟ Who found the key?

ما* اسْمُكَ؟ What is your name?   لِماذا تَصيح؟ Why are you shouting?

كَيْف أُمُّكَ؟ How is your mother?   بِكَم الآلة؟ How much is the machine?

*maadhaa is followed by a verb, maa by a noun.

Relative clauses

The Arabic relative pronouns ("which/who") are:

اَلَّذِي (*aladhii*) masculine sing.   اَلَّذِينَ (*aladhiina*) masculine pl.

اَلَّتِي (*alatii*) feminine sing.   اَللَاتِي (*allaatii*) feminine pl.

Pay particular attention to the difference between these two clauses:

المُلاكِم الذي أختارَ المُدَرِّب the boxer who chose the trainer

المُلاكِم الذي أختارَهُ المُدَرِّب the boxer whom the trainer chose [him]

If the second sentence is indefinite, the relative pronoun is left out:

مُلاكِم أختارَهُ المُدَرِّب a boxer whom the trainer chose [him]

28 The dual

Arabic has a separate form for talking about <u>two</u> things: the *dual* form. This is less common than the *singular* (<u>one</u> thing) or the *plural* (<u>three or more</u> things), and for this reason it has been separated from the main chapters. Having said that, you will come across the dual sometimes and may have to use it occasionally, so you need to know the basics of how it works.

The dual in general is characterized by a long *aa*. Look at the dual words for "you" and "they:"

أَنْتُمـا (*'antumaa*) you two [*masculine* and *feminine*]

هُمـا (*humaa*) they two [*masculine* and *feminine*]

If you want to refer to two people or things (*nouns*), you add the dual ending ـان (*aani*). (This ending changes to ـَين (*-ayni*) in the accusative and genitive case — see Appendix (ii).) If the nouns end with *taa' marbuuTa*, this is fully pronounced when you add the ending:

كِتاب (*kitaab*) book → كِتابانِ (*kitaabaani*) two books

مَدينة (*madiina*) city → مَدينتانِ (*madiinataani*) two cities

The dual ending is also added to adjectives:

هُمـا مَشْغولانِ They (two) are busy.

هُنـاكَ مُمَرِّضَتانِ جَديدتانِ في المُسْتَشْفَى.
There are two new nurses in the hospital.

There are also special verb endings for the dual. You can find these in Chapter 17.

Appendix (i)
Arabic alphabet and pronunciation

Here are the Arabic letters in alphabetical order with the transliteration used in this book, together with the vowels and dipthongs ([S] = sun letter, see 105–6).

Letters of the alphabet:

ا ('alif) *used for vowel sounds*

ب (baa') *b*, as in "bat"

ت (taa') *t*, as in "tank" [S]

ث (thaa') *th*, as in "this" [S]

ج (jiim) *j*, as in French "bonjour"

ح (Haa') *H*, strong breathy *h*

خ (khaa') *kh*, as in Scottish "loch"

د (daal) *d*, as in "dad" [S]

ذ (dhaal) *dh*, as in "that" [S]

ر (raa') *r*, as in "rain" [S]

ز (zay) *z*, as in "zero" [S]

س (siin) *s*, as in "sorry" [S]

ش (shiin) *sh*, as in "shut" [S]

ص (Saad) *S*, strong, emphatic *s* [S]

ض (Daad) *D*, strong, emphatic *d* [S]

ط (Taa') *T*, strong, emphatic *t* [S]

ظ (Zaa') *Z*, strong, emphatic *z* [S]

ع (ع ayn) ع, guttural stop

غ (ghayn) *gh*, as in French "maigret"

ف (faa') *f*, as in "fall"

ق (qaaf) *q*, said from back of throat

ك (kaaf) *k*, as in "kate"

ل (laam) *l*, as in "letter" [S]

م (miim) *m*, as in "met"

ن (nuun) *n*, as in "never" [S]

ه (haa') *h*, as in "hand"

و (waaw) *w*, as in "wand"

ي (yaa') *y*, as in "yellow"

ء (hamza) ', short pause/stop (1)

short vowels:

ـَ (fatHa) *a*, as in "mat"

ـُ (Damma) *u*, as in "sugar"

ـِ (kasra) *i*, as in "bit"

long vowels:

ـَا *aa*, as in "far" (2)

ـُو *uu*, as in "boot"

ـِي *ii*, as in "meet"

dipthongs:

ـَوْ *aw*, as in "how" or "home"

ـَيْ *ay*, as in "lie"

(1) Note that that there is a special type of *hamza* found at the beginning of the word *al* ("the") and a few other words. This is called *hamza al-waSl* ("the joining hamza"). It is not usually written and the vowel it carries elides when preceded by another vowel:

الْبَيْت (*al-bayt* – "the house") but وَجَدوا الْبَيْت (*wajaduu l-bayt* – "they found the house")

(2) Occasionally, *aa* is written using a *yaa'* (without dots) rather than an *'alif*. This always happens at the end of a word and is called *'alif maqsuura*: على (ع *alaa*– "on").

Appendix (ii)
Grammatical case endings

Many languages — German, for example — have grammatical cases that affect the noun endings. Arabic has three cases — nominative, accusative and genitive. However, the case endings are not usually pronounced in Modern Arabic, nor do they generally affect the spelling. Situations where you might hear them include high-level academic discussions (on TV, for example), recitations of the Quran or other religious and literary texts, or sometimes as a kind of flourish at the end of a sentence. Most beginning and intermediate learners can gloss over this aspect of Arabic grammar. However, it is useful to know that these cases exist and to have some idea of how they work so you are not thrown when you do meet them.

The following table shows how the three cases work for most nouns in the definite and indefinite. The underlining shows the case ending. The ending in bold— the extra accusative *'alif* — affects the basic spelling and you should try to remember this.

	nominative	accusative	genitive
indefinite	بيتٌ (*baytun*)	بيتاً (*baytan*)	بيتٍ (*baytin*)
definite	البيتُ (*al-baytu*)	البيتَ (*al-bayta*)	البيتِ (*al-bayti*)

The most important uses of the cases are listed below, but this is just an indication. For more information, consult a detailed Arabic grammar book.
  • *nominative*: for the subject of a sentence
  • *accusative*: for the object of a verb
  • *genitive*: after prepositions
          for the second noun in an *'idafa* (see page 119)

There are exceptions to the endings given above. The most common of these is the sound masculine plural:

	nominative	accusative	genitive
indefinite	مُدَرِّسونَ (*mudarrisuuna*)	مُدَرِّسينَ (*mudarrisiina*)	مُدَرِّسينَ (*mudarrisiina*)
definite*	المُدَرِّسونَ (*al-mudarrisuuna*)	المُدَرِّسينَ (*al-mudarrisiina*)	المُدَرِّسينَ (*al-mudarrisiina*)

* The final *nuun* is dropped in an *'idaafa* construction — see page 119.

Appendix (iii) Numbers

Here are the Arabic numbers, as numerals and spelled out. Arabic numbers are complex. The most important aspects are noted at the bottom of the page, but you will need a full grammar book to cover all the idiosyncrasies.

واحِد ١ (*waaHid*) – 1

إِثْنان ٢ (*ithnaan*) – 2

ثَلاثة ٣ (*thalaatha*) – 3

أَرْبَعة ٤ (*'arbaɛa*) – 4

خَمْسة ٥ (*khamsa*) – 5

سِتّة ٦ (*sitta*) – 6

سَبْعة ٧ (*sabɛa*) – 7

ثَمانية ٨ (*thamaaniya*) – 8

تِسْعة ٩ (*tisɛa*) – 9

عَشَرة ١٠ (*ɛashara*) – 10

أَحَد عَشَر ١١ (*'ahad ɛashar*) – 11

إِثْنا عَشَر ١٢ (*ithnaa ɛashar*) – 12

ثَلاثة عَشَر ١٣ (*thalaathat ɛashar*) – 13

أَرْبَعة عَشَر ١٤ (*'arbaɛat ɛashar*) – 14

خَمْسة عَشَر ١٥ (*khamsat ɛashar*) – 15

سِتّة عَشَر ١٦ (*sittat ɛashar*) – 16

سَبْعة عَشَر ١٧ (*sabɛat ɛashar*) – 17

ثَمانية عَشَر ١٨ (*thamaaniyat ɛashar*) – 18

تِسْعة عَشَر ١٩ (*tisɛat ɛashar*) – 19

عِشْرون ٢٠ (*ɛishruun*) – 20

واحِد وَعِشْرون ٢١ (*waaHid wa ɛishruun*) – 21

إِثْنان وَعِشْرون ٢٢ (*ithnaan wa ɛishruun*) – 22

ثَلاثون ٣٠ (*thalaathuun*) – 30

أَرْبَعون ٤٠ (*'arbaɛuun*) – 40

خَمْسون ٥٠ (*khamsuun*) – 50

سِتّون ٦٠ (*sittuun*) – 60

سَبْعون ٧٠ (*sabɛuun*) – 70

ثَمانون ٨٠ (*thamaanuun*) – 80

تِسْعون ٩٠ (*tisɛuun*) – 90

مِئة ١٠٠ (*mi'a*) – 100

أَلْف ١٠٠٠ (*'alf*) – 1,000

مِلْيون ١٠٠٠٠٠٠ (*milyuun*) – 1,000,000

Note:

- Arabic numerals are written left to right (see above).
- The numbers above are those you will meet most often. However, there are some changes if followed by a *feminine* noun, notably the numbers 3–9 will lose the ة (*taa' marbuuta*): ثَلاث بَنات 3 girls; ثَلاثة أَوْلاد 3 boys.
- Numbers 3–9 are followed by a *plural* noun, but 11 upwards by a *singular* noun (in the accusative — see Appendix (ii): ثَلاثة كُتُب 3 books; ثَلاثون كِتابًا 30 books.

Verb Index:

400 Arabic verbs for easy reference

This two-part *Arabic–English* and *English–Arabic* index contains all the verbs in the book, together with over 200 further high-frequency Arabic verbs.

Many Arabic references arrange verbs according to root letters and/or type. However, for many learners identifying the root and the type of verb can itself be the main difficulty. So the Arabic–English section of this glossary is presented in strict Arabic alphabetical order (*past tense* followed by *present*). You'll find the Arabic letters in alphabetical order on page 124. By using this system of alphabetization, you can look up an individual verb and find out its root letters, pronunciation, type and meaning. You can then look up how the verb behaves in the different tenses by using the references to conjugation tables in the main book.

The English meanings given here are not intended to be comprehensive. There may be alternative meanings or nuances for a particular verb that are not possible to include in this type of index. Once you have established the root letters and type of verb, you can clarify the meaning in a good dictionary (see pages 8–9).

We have also included below a further table showing where you can find other verbal formations. For example, once you have established from the index that the verb درّس، يدرّس *darrasa, yudarris* is Form II you can then go to the table below and find the page reference for the formation and use of the passive, subjunctive, jussive (including imperative), verbal nouns, and participles for this type of verb.

	Form I (Basic)	Forms II–X	Quadriliteral
Passive	82–84	85	—
Subjunctive	66–67	66–67	—
Jussive	70–75	70–75	—
Verbal noun	87–88	88	97
Active participle	91	92	97
Passive participle	91	92	97

← *Read this way*

Page reference	English	Verb Type	Transliteration	Root	Arabic verb
					ا
60	be sad	*VIII, hamzated*	ibta'asa, yabta'is	ب ء س	ابتأس، يبتئس
60	begin	*VIII, hamzated*	ibtada'a, yabtadi'	ب د ء	ابتدأ، يبتدئ
57–58 (as iqtaraba, yaqtarib)	smile	*VIII, regular*	ibtasama, yabtasim	ب س م	ابتسم، يبتسم
57–58 (as istaعlama, yastaعlim)	receive (guests, etc.)	*X, regular*	istaqbala, yastaqbil	ق ب ل	استقبل، يستقبل
60 (as istawqafa, yastawqif)	import	*X, assimilated*	istawrada, yastawrid	و ر د	استورد، يستورد
60	adopt (measures, etc.)	*VIII, hamzated*	ittakhadha, yattakhidh	ء خ ذ	اتّخذ، يتّخذ
60 (as ittafaqa, yattafiq)	contact	*VIII, assimilated*	ittaSala, yattaSil	و ص ل	اتّصل، يتّصل
60	agree	*VIII, assimilated*	ittafaqa, yattafiq	و ق ف	اتّفق، يتّفق
57–58 (as iqtaraba, yaqtarib)	meet	*VIII, regular*	ijtamaعa, yajtamiع	ج م ع	اجتمع، يجتمع
57–58 (as iqtaraba, yaqtarib)	work hard	*VIII, regular*	ijtahada, yajtahid	ج ه د	اجتهد، يجتهد
60	need	*VIII, hollow*	iHtaaja, yaHtaaj	ح و ج	احتاج، يحتاج
57–58 (as iqtaraba, yaqtarib)	respect	*VIII, regular*	iHtarama, yaHtarim	ح ر م	احترم، يحترم
57–58 (as iqtaraba, yaqtarib)	celebrate	*VIII, regular*	iHtafala, yaHtafil	ح ف ل	احتفل، يحتفل
60 (as imtadda, yamtadd)	occupy (land, etc.)	*VIII, doubled*	iHtalla, yaHtall	ح ل ل	احتلّ، يحتلّ
60 (as ishtaraa, yashtarii)	contain	*VIII, defective*	iHtawaa, yaHtawii	ح و ي	احتوى، يحتوي
54	turn red	*IX, regular*	iHmarra, yaHmarr	ح م ر	احمرّ، يحمرّ
60 (as iHtaaja, yaHtaaj)	choose	*VIII, hollow*	ikhtaara, yakhtaar	خ ي ر	اختار، يختار
57–58 (as iqtaraba, yaqtarib)	shorten	*VIII, regular*	ikhtaSara, yakhtaSir	خ ص ر	اختصر، يختصر
55	save, store	*VIII, irregular*	iddakhara, yaddakhir	د خ ر	اذّخر، يدّخر
60 (as ishtaraa, yashtarii)	put on (clothes)	*VIII, defective*	irtadaa, yartadii	ر د ي	ارتدى، يرتدي
57–58 (as iqtaraba, yaqtarib)	rise	*VIII, regular*	irtafaعa, yartafiع	ر ف ع	ارتفع، يرتفع
55	crowd	*VIII, irregular*	izdaHama, yazdaHim	ز ح م	ازدحم، يزدحم
60	rent, hire	*X, hamzated*	ista'jara, yasta'jir	ء ج ر	استأجر، يستأجر
60 (as ista'jara, yasta'jir)	ask for permission	*X, hamzated*	ista'dhana, yasta'dhin	ء ذ ن	استأذن، يستأذن
60	exclude	*X, defective*	istathnaa, yastathnii	ث ن ي	استثنى، يستثني
57–58 (as istaعlama, yastaعlim)	admire	*X, regular*	istaHsana, yastaHsin	ح س ن	استحسن، يستحسن

← ——————— *Read this way*

Page reference	English	Verb Type	Transliteration	Root	Arabic verb
60 (as istamarra, yastamirr)	deserve	X, doubled	istaHaqqa, yastaHiqq	ح ق ق	استحقّ، يستحقّ
60 (as istamarra, yastamirr)	bathe	X, doubled	istaHamma, yastaHimm	ح م م	استحمّ، يستحمّ
57–58 (as istaعlama, yastaعlim)	use, employ	X, regular	istakhdama, yastakhdim	خ د م	استخدم، يستخدم
57–58 (as istaعlama, yastaعlim)	extract	X, regular	istakhraja, yastakhrij	خ ر ج	استخرج، يستخرج
60 (as istaqaala, yastaqiil)	rest, relax	X, hollow	istaraaHa, yastariiH	ر و ح	استراح، يستريح
60 (as istaqaala, yastaqiil)	be able to	X, hollow	istaTaaعa, yastaTiiع	ط و ع	استطاع، يستطيع
57–58	enquire	X, regular	istaعlama, yastaعlim	ع ل م	استعلم، يستعلم
57–58 (as istaعlama, yastaعlim)	utilize	X, regular	istaعmala, yastaعmil	ع م ل	استعمل، يستعمل
60	resign	X, hollow	istaqaala, yastaqiil	ق ي ل	استقال، يستقيل
57–58 (as istaعlama, yastaعlim)	explore	X, regular	istakshafa, yastakshif	ك ش ف	استكشف، يستكشف
57–58 (as istaعlama, yastaعlim)	enjoy	X, regular	istamtaعa, yastamtiع	م ت ع	استمتع، يستمتع
60	continue	X, doubled	istamarra, yastamirr	م ر ر	استمرّ، يستمرّ
57–58 (as iqtaraba, yaqtarib)	listen	VIII, regular	istamaعa, yastamiع	س م ع	استمع، يستمع
60	mock, make fun of	X, hamzated	istahza'a, yastahzi'	ه ز ء	استهزأ، يستهزئ
60	stop (someone)	X, assimilated	istawqafa, yastawqif	و ق ف	استوقف، يستوقف
60 (as istawqafa, yastawqif)	wake, awaken	X, assimilated	istayqaZa, yastayqiZ	ي ق ظ	استيقظ، يستيقظ
57–58 (as iqtaraba, yaqtarib)	participate	VIII, regular	ishtaraka, yashtarik	ش ر ك	اشترك، يشترك
60	buy	VIII, defective	ishtaraa, yashtarii	ش ر ي	اشترى، يشتري
55–56	be disturbed	VIII, irregular	iDTaraba, yaDTarib	ض ر ب	اضطرب، يضطرب
55–56	be informed about	VIII, irregular	iTTalaعa, yaTTaliع	ط ل ع	اطّلع، يطّلع
60 (as iHtaaja, yaHtaaj)	be accustomed to	VIII, hollow	iعtanda, yaعtaud	ع و د	اعتاد، يعتاد
57–58 (as iqtaraba, yaqtarib)	apologize	VIII, regular	iعtadhara, yaعtadhir	ع ذ ر	اعتذر، يعتذر
57–58 (as iqtaraba, yaqtarib)	believe	VIII, regular	iعtaqada, yaعtaqid	ع ق د	اعتقد، يعتقد
57–58	approach, advance	VIII, regular	iqtaraba, yaqtarib	ق ر ب	اقترب، يقترب
42–43 (as darrasa, yudarris)	borrow	VIII, regular	iqtaraDa, yaqtariD	ق ر ض	اقترض، يقترض
98	shudder, quake	IV, quadriliteral	iqshaعarra, yaqshaعirr	ق ش ع ر	اقشعرّ، يقشعرّ
60 (as iHtaaja, yaHtaaj)	be differentiated	VIII, hollow	imtaaza, yamtaaz	م ي ز	امتاز، يمتاز
57–58 (as iqtaraba, yaqtarib)	examine	VIII, regular	imtaHana, yamtaHin	م ح ن	امتحن، يمتحن

⟵ *Read this way*

Page reference	English	Verb Type	Transliteration	Root	Arabic verb
60	extend	VIII, doubled	imtadda, yamtadd	م د د	امتدّ ، يمتدّ
57–58 (as iqtaraba, yaqtarib)	stop, desist	VIII, regular	imtanaع a, yamtaniع	م ن ع	امتنع ، يمتنع
57–58 (as iqtaraba, yaqtarib)	pay attention	VIII, regular	intabaha, yantabih	ن ب ه	انتبه ، ينتبه
57–58 (as iqtaraba, yaqtarib)	become widespread	VIII, regular	intashara, yantashir	ن ش ر	انتشر ، ينتشر
57–58 (as iqtaraba, yaqtarib)	wait	VIII, regular	intaZara, yantaZir	ن ظ ر	انتظر ، ينتظر
60 (as ishtaraa, yashtarii)	finish, end	VIII, defective	intahaa, yantahii	ن ه ي	انتهى ، ينتهي
60	bow, wind	VII, defective	inHanaa, yanHanii	ن ح و	انحنى ، ينحني
57–58 (as inqalaba, yanqalib)	withdraw	VII, regular	insaHaba, yansaHib	س ح ب	انسحب ، ينسحب
57–58 (as inqalaba, yanqalib)	depart	VII, regular	inSarafa, yanSarif	ص ر ف	انصرف ، ينصرف
60	join, enroll	VII, doubled	inDamma, yanDamm	ض م م	انضمّ ، ينضمّ
60	be led	VII, hollow	inqaada, yanqaad	ق و د	انقاد ، ينقاد
60	be read	VII, hamzated	inqara'a, yanqari'	ق ر ء	انقرأ ، ينقرئ
57–58 (as inqalaba, yanqalib)	be divided	VII, regular	inqasama, yanqasim	ق س م	انقسم ، ينقسم
60 (as inHanaa, yanHanii)	be finished	VII, defective	inqaDaa, yanqaDii	ق ض ي	انقضى ، ينقضي
57–58	turn over, capsize	VII, regular	inqalaba, yanqalib	ق ل ب	انقلب ، ينقلب
57–58 (as inqalaba, yanqalib)	be broken	VII, regular	inkasara, yankasir	ك س ر	انكسر ، ينكسر
45	blame	III, hamzated	'aakhadha, yu'aakhidh	ء خ ذ	آخذ ، يؤاخذ
45 (as 'aamana, yu'min)	hurt	IV, hamzated	'aalama, yu'lim	ء ل م	آلم ، يؤلم
45	believe (in)	IV, hamzated	'aamana, yu'min	ء م ن	آمن ، يؤمن
27–28 (as mashaa, yamshii)	come	I, defective, hamzated	'ataa, ya'tii	ء ت ي	أتى ، يأتي
45	influence	II, hamzated	'aththara, yu'aththir	ء ث ر	أثّر ، يؤثّر
45 (as 'araada, yuriid)	answer	IV, hollow	'ajaaba, yajiib	ج و ب	أجاب ، يجيب
45 (as 'aththara, yu'aththir)	rent, hire	II, hamzated	'ajjara, yu'ajjir	ء ج ر	أجّر ، يؤجّر
45	like, love	IV, doubled	'aHabba, yuHibb	ح ب ب	أحبّ ، يحبّ
42–43 (as 'aع lama, yuع lim)	do well	IV, regular	aHsana, yuHsin	ح س ن	أحسن ، يحسن
42–43 (as 'aع lama, yuع lim)	inform, tell	IV, regular	'akhbara, yukhbir	خ ب ر	أخبر ، يخبر
35-36	take	I, hamzated	'akhadha, ya'khudh	ء خ ذ	أخذ ، يأخذ

Page reference	English	Verb Type	Transliteration	Root	Arabic verb
42–43 (as 'aعlama, yuعlim)	remove	IV, regular	'akhraja, yukhrij	خ ر ج	أخرج، يخرج
45 (as 'araada, yuriid)	turn (something), manage (e.g. business)	IV, hollow	'adaara, yudiir	د و ر	أدار، يدير
35–36 (as 'akhadha, ya'khudh)	permit	I, hamzated	'adhina, ya'dhan	ء ذ ن	أذن، يأذن
45	want	IV, hollow	'araada, yuriid	ر و د	أراد، يريد
42–43 (as 'aعlama, yuعlim)	send	IV, regular	'arsala, yursil	ر س ل	أرسل، يرسل
45	bore (someone)	IV, hamzated	'as'ama, yu'sim	س ء م	أسأم، يسئم
42–43 (as 'aعlama, yuعlim)	hurry	IV, regular	'asraعa, yusriع	س ر ع	أسرع، يسرع
35–36 (as 'akhadha, ya'khudh)	regret	I, hamzated	'asifa, ya'saf	ء س ف	أسف، يأسف
45 (as 'aththara, yu'aththir)	establish, found	II, doubled, hamzated	'assasa, yu'assis	ء س س	أسّس، يؤسّس
45 (as 'araada, yuriid)	point, indicate	IV, hollow	'ashaara, yushiir	ش و ر	أشار، يشير
42–43 (as 'aعlama, yuعlim)	become	IV, regular	'aSbaHa, yuSbiH	ص ب ح	أصبح، يصبح
45 (as 'aHabba, yuHibb)	insist	IV, doubled	'aSarra, yuSirr	ص ر ر	أصرّ، يصرّ
42–43 (as 'aعlama, yuعlim)	repair	IV, regular	'aSlaHa, yuSliH	ص ل ح	أصلح، يصلح
45 (as 'araada, yuriid)	add	IV, hollow	'aDaafa, yuDiif	ض ي ف	أضاف، يضيف
45 (as 'ansha'a, yunshi')	extinguish	IV, hamzated	'aTfa'a, yuTfi'	ط ف ء	أطفأ، يطفئ
42–43 (as 'aعlama, yuعlim)	set off, liberate	IV, regular	'aTlaqa, yaTliq	ط ل ق	أطلق، يطلق
45 (as 'araada, yuriid)	lend	IV, hollow	'aعaara, yuعiir	ع و ر	أعار، يعير
45 (as 'aHabba, yuHibb)	prepare	IV, doubled	'aعadda, yuعidd	ع د د	أعدّ، يعدّ
45	give	IV, defective	'aعTaa, yuعTii	ع ط و	أعطى، يعطي
42–43	inform	IV, regular	'aعlama, yuعlim	ع ل م	أعلم، يعلم
45 (as 'araada, yuriid)	benefit	IV, hollow	'afaada, yufiid	ف ي د	أفاد، يفيد
42–43 (as 'aعlama, yuعlim)	take off	IV, regular	'aqlaعa, yuqliع	ق ل ع	أقلع، يقلع
35–36 (as 'akhadha, ya'khudh)	eat	I, hamzated	'akala, ya'kul	ء ك ل	أكل، يأكل
45 (as 'aththara, yu'aththir)	confirm	II, hamzated	'akkada, yu'akkid	ء ك د	أكّد، يؤكّد
35–36 (as 'akhadha, ya'khudh)	command	I, hamzated	'amara, ya'mur	ء م ر	أمر، يأمر
35–36 (as 'akhadha, ya'khudh)	hope	I, hamzated	'amala, ya'mul	ء م ل	أمل، يأمل
45	construct, found	IV, hamzated	'ansha'a, yunshi'	ن ش ء	أنشأ، ينشئ
42–43 (as 'aعlama, yuعlim)	refresh	IV, regular	'anعasha, yunعish	ن ع ش	أنعش، ينعش

⟵ *Read this way*

Page reference	English	Verb Type	Transliteration	Root	Arabic verb
45 (as 'aɛTaa, yuɛTii)	finish	IV, defective	'anhaa, yunhii	ن ه ي	أنهى، ينهي
45 (as 'awSala, yuuSil)	deposit	IV, assimilated	'awdaɛa, yuudiɛ	و د ع	أودع، يودع
45	connect	IV, assimilated	'awSala, yuuSil	و ص ل	أوصل، يوصل

ب

23–25 (as Taara, yaTiir)	sell	I, hollow	baaɛa, yabiiɛ	ب ي ع	باع، يبيع
13–17	search	I, regular	baHatha, yabHath	ب ح ث	بحث، يبحث
27–28 (as shakaa, yashkuu)	seem, appear	I, defective	badaa, yabduu	ب د و	بدا، يبدو
35–36 (as qara'a, yaqra')	begin	I, hamzated	bada'a, yabda'	ب د ء	بدأ، يبدأ
13–17	be/go cold	I, regular	barada, yabrad	ب ر د	برد، يبرد
35-36	be slow	I, hamzated	baTu'a, yabTu'	ب ط ء	بطؤ، يبطؤ
27–28 (as nasiya, yansaa)	remain, stay	I, defective	baqiya, yabqaa	ب ق ي	بقي، يبقى
27–28 (as mashaa, yamshii)	weep	I, defective	bakaa, yabkee	ب ك ي	بكى، يبكي
13–17	swallow	I, regular	balaɛa, yablaɛ	ع ل ع	بلع، يبلع
13–17	reach	I, regular	balagha, yablugh	ب ل غ	بلغ، يبلغ
27–28 (as mashaa, yamshii)	build	I, defective	banaa, yabnii	ن ن ي	بنى، يبني

ت

23–25 (as zaara, yazuur)	get lost	I, hollow	taaha, yatuuh	ت و ه	تاه، يتوه
52	be familiar	VI, hamzated	ta'aalafa, yata'aalaf	ء ل ف	تآلف، يتآلف
52	be influenced	V, hamzated	ta'aththara, yata'aththar	ء ث ر	تأثّر، يتأثّر
52 (as ta'aththara, yata'aththar)	be late	V, hamzated	ta'akhkhara, yata'akhkhar	ء خ ر	تأخّر، يتأخّر
13–17	follow	I, regular	tabaɛa, yatbaɛ	ت ب ع	تبع، يتبع
42–43 (as darrasa, yudarris)	season (food)	II, regular	tabbala, yutabbil	ت ب ل	تبّل، يتبّل
52 (as talawwana, yatalawwan)	wander	V, hollow	tajawwala, yatajawwal	ج و ل	تجوّل، يتجوّل
49–50	converse	VI, regular	taHaadatha, yataHaadath	ح د ث	تحادث، يتحادث
49–50 (as tadhakkara, yatadhakkar)	talk, speak	V, regular	taHaddatha, yataHaddath	ح د ث	تحدّث، يتحدّث
49–50 (as tadhakkara, yatadhakkar)	move	V, regular	taHarraka, yataHarrak	ح ر ك	تحرّك، يتحرّك
49–50 (as tadhakkara, yatadhakkar)	improve	V, regular	taHassana, yataHassan	ح س ن	تحسّن، يتحسّن

Page reference	English	Verb Type	Transliteration	Root	Arabic verb
49–50	remember	V, regular	tadhakkara, yatadhakkar	ذ ك ر	تذكّر، يتذكّر
97 (as daHraja, yudaHrij)	translate	I, quadriliteral	tarjama, yutarjim	ت ر ج م	ترجم، يترجم
52	hesitate	V, doubled	taraddada, yataraddad	ر د د	تردّد، يتردّد
13–17	leave, abandon	I, regular	taraka, yatruk	ت ر ك	ترك، يترك
52 (as talawwana, yatalawwan)	marry, get married	V, hollow	tazawwaja, yatazawwaj	ز و ج	تزوّج، يتزوّج
52	wonder	VI, hamzated	tasaa'ala, yatasaa'al	س ء ل	تساءل، يتساءل
98 (as tafalsafa, yatafalsaf)	follow one another	II, quadriliteral	tasalsala, yatasalsal	س ل س ل	تسلسل، يتسلسل
49–50 (as tadhakkara, yatadhakkar)	climb	V, regular	tasallaqa, yatasallaq	س ل ق	تسلّق، يتسلّق
52 (as tamannaa, yatamannaa)	be amused	V, defective	tasallaa, yatasallaa	س ل و	تسلّى، يتسلّى
52 (as talawwana, yatalawwan)	shop, go shopping	V, hollow	tasawwaqa, yatasawwaq	س و ق	تسوّق، يتسوّق
49–50 (as tadhakkara, yatadhakkar)	behave	V, regular	taSarrafa, yataSarraf	ص ر ف	تصرّف، يتصرّف
52 (as talawwana, yatalawwan)	imagine	V, hollow	taSawwara, yataSawwar	ص و ر	تصوّر، يتصوّر
52 (as taعaawana, yataعaawan)	be annoyed	VI, hollow	taDaayaqa, yataDaayaq	ض ي ق	تضايق، يتضايق
52	cooperate	VI, hollow	taعaawana, yataعaawan	ع و ن	تعاون، يتعاون
13–17	tire, wear out	I, regular	taعiba, yatعab	ت ع ب	تعب، يتعب
52 (as tamannaa, yatamannaa)	dine, have dinner	V, defective	taعashshaa, yataعashshaa	ع ش ي	تعشّى، يتعشّى
49–50 (as tadhakkara, yatadhakkar)	put on perfume	V, regular	taعaTTara, yataعaTTar	ع ط ر	تعطّر، يتعطّر
49–50 (as tadhakkara, yatadhakkar)	learn	V, regular	taعallama, yataعallam	ع ل م	تعلّم، يتعلّم
52 (as tamannaa, yatamannaa)	have lunch	V, defective	taghaddaa, yataghaddaa	غ د و	تغدّى، يتغدّى
49–50 (as taHaadatha, yataHaadath)	be dispersed	VI, regular	tafaaraqa, yatafaaraq	ف ر ق	تفارق، يتفارق
52	be optimisitc	V, hamzated	tafa''ala, yatafa''al	ف ء ل	تفأّل، يتفأّل
98	philosophize	II, quadriliteral	tafalsafa, yatafalsaf	ف ل س ف	تفلسف، يتفلسف
49–50 (as tadhakkara, yatadhakkar)	excel	V, regular	tafawwaqa, yatafawwaq	ف و ق	تفوّق، يتفوّق
49–50 (as taHaadatha, yataHaadath)	be lazy	VI, regular	takaasala, yatakaasal	ك س ل	تكاسل، يتكاسل

◄──────── *Read this way*

age reference	English	Verb Type	Transliteration	Root	Arabic verb
	be equal	VI, hamzated	takaafa'a, yatakaafa'	ك ف ء	تكافأ ، يتكافأ
49–50 (as tadhakkara, yatadhakkar)	talk	V, regular	takallama, yatakallam	ك ل م	تكلّم ، يتكلّم
52	meet up	VI, defective	talaaqaa, yatalaaqaa	ل ق ي	تلاقى ، يتلاقى
49–50 (as tadhakkara, yatadhakkar)	be polluted	V, regular	talawwatha, yatalawwath	ل و ث	تلوّث ، يتلوّث
52	be colored	V, hollow	talawwana, yatalawwan	ل و ن	تلوّن ، يتلوّن
97	mutter	I, quadriliteral	tamtama, yutamtim	ت م ت م	تمتم ، يتمتم
52	wish, want	V, defective	tamannaa, yatamannaa	م ن و	تمنّى ، يتمنّى
31 (as radda, yarudd)	be finished	I, doubled	tamma, yatimm	ت م م	تمّ ، يتمّ
52	predict	V, hamzated	tanabba'a, yatanabba'	ن ب ء	تنبّأ ، يتنبّأ
52	agree together	VI, assimilated	tawaafaqa, yatawaafaq	و ف ق	توافق ، يتوافق
52	expect	V, assimilated	tawaqqaعa, yatawaqqaعa	و ق ع	توقّع ، يتوقّع
52 (tawaqqaعa, yatawaqqaعa)	stop	V, assimilated	tawaqqafa, yatawaqqaf	و ق ف	توقّف ، يتوقّف

ث

| 97 | chatter | I, quadriliteral | tharthara, yutharthir | ث ر ث ر | ثرثر ، يثرثر |

ج

99	come	I, hollow, hamzated	jaa'a, yajii'	ج ي ء	جاء ، يجيء
42–43 (as saabaqa, yusaabiq)	argue	III, regular	jaadala, yajaadil	ج د ل	جادل ، يجادل
27–28 (as mashaa, yamshii)	run	I, defective	jaraa, yajrii	ج ر ي	جرى ، يجري
13–17	sit	I, regular	jalasa, yajlis	ج ل س	جلس ، يجلس
13–17	collect	I, regular	jamaعa, yajmaع	ج م ع	جمع ، يجمع
42–43 (as darrasa, yudarris)	prepare	II, regular	jahhaza, yujahhiz	ج ه ز	جهّز ، يجهّز

ح

42–43 (as saabaqa, yusaabiq)	talk to	III, regular	Haadatha, yuHaadith	ح د ث	حادث ، يحادث
45 (as naawala, yunaawil)	try	III, hollow	Haawala, yuHaawil	ح و ل	حاول ، يحاول
13–17	reserve	I, regular	Hajaza, yaHjiz	ح ج ز	حجز ، يحجز
13–17	happen	I, regular	Hadatha, yaHduth	ح د ث	حدث ، يحدث
13–17	burn	I, regular	Haraqa, yaHriq	ح ر ق	حرق ، يحرق

◄────── *Read this way*

Page reference	English	Verb Type	Transliteration	Root	Arabic verb
					ذ
23–25 (as zaara, yazuur)	taste	I, hollow	dhaaqa, yadhuuq	ذ و ق	ذاق، يذوق
42–43 (as saabaqa, yusaabiq)	study	III, regular	dhaakara, yudhaakir	ذ ك ر	ذاكر، يذاكر
13–17	mention	I, regular	dhakara, yadhkur	ذ ك ر	ذكر، يذكر
42–43 (as darrasa, yudarris)	remind	II, regular	dhakkara, yudhakkir	ذ ك ر	ذكّر، يذكّر
13–17	go	I, regular	dhahaba, yadh-hab	ذ ه ب	ذهب، يذهب
					ر
100	see	I, defective, hamzated	ra'aa, yaraa	ر ء ي	رأى، يرى
13–17	win	I, regular	rabaHa, yarbaH	ر ب ح	ربح، يربح
45	breed, raise	II, defective	rabbaa, yurabbii	ر ب و	ربّى، يربّي
42–43 (as darrasa, yudarris)	arrange, tidy	II, regular	rattaba, yurattib	ر ت ب	رتّب، يرتّب
27–28 (as shakaa, yashkuu)	request, hope	I, defective	rajaa, yarjuu	ر ج و	رجا، يرجو
13–17	return	I, regular	rajaعa, yarjaع	ر ج ع	رجع، يرجع
42–43 (as darrasa, yudarris)	welcome	II, regular	raHHaba, yuraHHib	ر ح ب	رحّب، يرحّب
31	reply, answer	I, doubled	radda, yarudd	ر د د	ردّ، يردّ
45	repeat	II, doubled	raddada, yuraddid	ر د د	ردّد، يردّد
13–17	draw (a picture)	I, regular	rasama, yarsum	ر س م	رسم، يرسم
27–28 (as nasiya, yansaa)	approve	I, defective	raDiya, yarDaa	ر ض ي	رضي، يرضى
13–17	refuse	I, regular	rafaDa, yarfuD	ر ف ض	رفض، يرفض
13–17	raise, lift up	I, regular	rafaعa, yarfaع	ر ف ع	رفع، يرفع
13–17	dance	I, regular	raqaSa, yarquS	ر ق ص	رقص، يرقص
13–17	ride, get on	I, regular	rakiba, yarkab	ر ك ب	ركب، يركب
27–28 (as mashaa, yamshii)	throw	I, defective	ramaa, yarmii	ر م ي	رمى، يرمي
23–25 (as Taara, yaTiir)	increase	I, hollow	zaada, yaziid	ز ي د	زاد، يزيد
23–25	visit	I, hollow	zaara, yazuur	ز و ر	زار، يزور
					ز
13–17	plant	I, regular	zaraعa, yazraع	ز ر ع	زرع، يزرع

Page reference	English	Verb Type	Transliteration	Root	Arabic verb
					س
45	question	*III, hamzated*	saa'ala, yusaa'il	س ء ل	ساءل، يسائل
42–43	race	*III, regular*	saabaqa, yusaabiq	س ب ق	سابق، يسابق
42–43 (as saabaqa, yusaabiq)	help	*III, regular*	saaعada, yusaaعid	س ع د	ساعد، يساعد
42–43 (as saabaqa, yusaabiq)	travel	*III, regular*	saafara, yusaafir	س ف ر	سافر، يسافر
45 (as laaqaa, yulaaqii)	equal	*III, defective*	saawaa, yusaawii	س و ي	ساوى، يساوي
35–36	ask	*I, hamzated*	sa'ala, yas'al	س ء ل	سأل، يسأل
13–17	swim	*I, regular*	sabaHa, yasbaH	س ب ح	سبح، يسبح
13–17	precede	*I, regular*	sabaqa, yasbiq	س ب ق	سبق، يسبق
45 (as raddada, yuraddid)	cause	*II, doubled*	sabbaba, yusabbib	س ب ب	سبّب، يسبّب
13–17	jail	*I, regular*	sajana, yasjun	س ج ن	سجن، يسجن
42–43 (as darrasa, yudarris)	record	*II, regular*	sajjala, yusajjil	س ج ل	سجّل، يسجّل
13–17	be hot	*I, regular*	sakhana, yaskhun	س خ ن	سخن، يسخن
42–43 (as darrasa, yudarris)	heat	*II, regular*	sakhkhana, yusakhkhin	س خ ن	سخّن، يسخّن
31 (as radda, yarudd)	block	*I, doubled*	sadda, yasudd	س د د	سدّ، يسدّ
13–17	steal	*I, regular*	saraqa, yasraq	س ر ق	سرق، يسرق
13–17	cough	*I, regular*	saعala, yasعul	س ع ل	سعل، يسعل
27–28 (as nasiya, yansaa)	attempt, strive	*I, defective*	saعiya, yasعaa	س ع ي	سعي، يسعى
13–17	fall	*I, regular*	saqaTa, yasquT	س ق ط	سقط، يسقط
13–17	live, reside	*I, regular*	sakana, yaskun	س ك ن	سكن، يسكن
13–17	allow	*I, regular*	samaHa, yasmaH	س م ح	سمح، يسمح
13–17	hear	*I, regular*	samiعa, yasmaع	س م ع	سمع، يسمع
45 (as rabbaa, yurabbii)	name	*II, defective*	sammaa, yusammii	س م ي	سمّى، يسمّي
35–36 (as sa'ala, yas'al)	be fed up	*I, hamzated*	sa'ima, yas'am	س ء م	سئم، يسأم
					ش
23–25 (as naama, yanaam)	want	*I, hollow, hamzated*	shaa'a, yashaa'	ش ي ء	شاء، يشاء
42–43 (as saabaqa, yusaabiq)	share (in), participate	*III, regular*	shaaraka, yushaarik	ش ر ك	شارك، يشارك

⟵ *Read this way*

Page reference	English	Verb Type	Transliteration	Root	Arabic verb
42–43 (as saabaqa, yusaabiq)	watch, view	*III, regular*	shaahada, yushaahid	ش ه د	شاهد، يشاهد
13–17	charge (battery, etc.)	*I, regular*	shaHana, yashHan	ش ح ن	شحن، يشحن
31 (as radda, yarudd)	strengthen, pull	*I, doubled*	shadda, yashidd	ش د د	شدّ، يشدّ
14–16 (as kataba, yaktub)	drink	*I, regular*	shariba, yashrab	ش ر ب	شرب، يشرب
13–17	feel	*I, regular*	shaعara, yashعur	ش ع ر	شعر، يشعر
27–28	complain	*I, defective*	shakaa, yashkuu	ش ك و	شكا، يشكو
13–17	thank	*I, regular*	shakara, yashkur	ش ك ر	شكر، يشكر
31 (as radda, yarudd)	doubt, suspect	*I, doubled*	shakka, yashukk	ش ك ك	شكّ، يشكّ
31 (as radda, yarudd)	smell	*I, doubled*	shamma, yashumm	ش م م	شمّ، يشمّ

ص

23–25 (as Taara, yaTiir)	shout	*I, hollow*	SaaHa, yaSiiH	ص ي ح	صاح، يصيح
23–25 (as Taara, yaTiir)	become	*I, hollow*	Saara, yaSiir	ص ي ر	صار، يصير
23–25 (as zaara, yazuur)	fast	*I, hollow*	Saama, yaSuum	ص و م	صام، يصوم
42–43 (as darrasa, yudarris)	believe	*II, regular*	Saddaqa, yuSSadiq	ص د ق	صدّق، يصدّق
42–43 (as darrasa, yudarris)	change (money, etc.)	*II, regular*	Sarrafa, yuSarrif	ص ر ف	صرّف، يصرّف
42–43 (as darrasa, yudarris)	repair	*II, regular*	SallaHa, yuSalliH	ص ل ح	صلّح، يصلّح
45 (as rabbaa, yurabbii)	pray	*II, defective*	Sallaa, yuSallii	ص ل و	صلّى، يصلّي
13–17	make, manufacture	*I, regular*	Sanaعa, yaSnaع	ص ن ع	صنع، يصنع
45 (as khawwafa, yukhawwif)	vote	*II, hollow*	Sawwata, yuSawwit	ص و ت	صوّت، يصوّت

ض

45	oppose	*III, doubled*	Daadd, yuDaadd	ض د د	ضادّ، يضادّ
13–17	laugh	*I, regular*	DaHika, yaDHak	ض ح ك	ضحك، يضحك
13–17	hit	*I, regular*	Daraba, yaDrub	ض ر ب	ضرب، يضرب

ط

23–25	fly	*I, hollow*	Taara, yaTiir	ط ي ر	طار، يطير
13–17	cook	*I, regular*	Tabakha, yaTbukh	ط ب خ	طبخ، يطبخ
13–17	print	*I, regular*	Tabaعa, yaTbaع	ط ب ع	طبع، يطبع
13–17	knock (on door, etc.)	*I, regular*	Taraqa, yaTruq	ط ر ق	طرق، يطرق

Page reference	English	Verb Type	Transliteration	Root	Arabic verb
97 (daHraja, yudaHrij)	crackle	I, quadriliteral	TaqTaqa, yuTaqTiq	ط ق ط ق	طقطق ، يطقطق
13–17	request	I, regular	Talaba, yaTlub	ط ل ب	طلب ، يطلب
					ظ
31 (as radda, yarudd)	think, imagine	I, doubled	Zanna, yaZunn	ظ ن ن	ظنّ ، يظنّ
13–17	appear	I, regular	Zahara, yaZhar	ظ ه ر	ظهر ، يظهر
					ع
23–25 (as zaara, yazuur)	return	I, hollow	ɛaada, yaɛuud	ع و د	عاد ، يعود
23–25 (as Taara, yaTiir)	live	I, hollow	ɛaasha, yaɛiish	ع ي ش	عاش ، يعيش
42–43 (as saabaqa, yusaabiq)	deal with	III, regular	ɛaamala, yuɛaamil	ع م ل	عامل ، يعامل
45 (as naawala, yunaawil)	help	III, hollow	ɛaawana, yuɛaawin	ع و ن	عاون ، يعاون
13–17	cross (road, etc.)	I, regular	ɛabara, yaɛbur	ع ب ر	عبر ، يعبر
31 (as radda, yarudd)	count	I, doubled	ɛadda, yaɛudd	ع د د	عدّ ، يعدّ
42–43 (as darrasa, yudarris)	adjust	II, regular	ɛaddala, yuɛaddil	ع د ل	عدّل ، يعدّل
13–17	display, show	I, regular	ɛaraDa, yaɛriD	ع ر ض	عرض ، يعرض
13–17	know	I, regular	ɛarafa, yaɛrif	ع ر ف	عرف ، يعرف
13–17	play (an instrument)	I, regular	ɛazafa, yaɛzif	ع ز ف	عزف ، يعزف
13–17	tie	I, regular	ɛaqada, yaɛqid	ع ق د	عقد ، يعقد
13–17	know	I, regular	ɛalima, yaɛlam	ع ل م	علم ، يعلم
42–43 (as darrasa, yudarris)	teach	II, regular	ɛallama, yuɛallim	ع ل م	علّم ، يعلّم
13–17	do, work	I, regular	ɛamila, yaɛmal	ع م ل	عمل ، يعمل
					غ
42–43 (as saabaqa, yusaabiq)	depart	III, regular	ghaadara, yughaadir	غ د ر	غادر ، يغادر
97	gargle	I, quadriliteral	gharghara, yugharghir	غ ر غ ر	غرغر ، يغرغر
13–17	wash	I, regular	ghasala, yaghsil	غ س ل	غسل ، يغسل
45 (as rabbaa, yurabbii)	cover	II, defective	ghaTTaa, yughaTTii	غ ط و	غطّى ، يغطّي
27–28 (as mashaa, yamshii)	boil	I, defective	ghalaa, yaghlii	غ ل ي	غلى ، يغلي
45 (as rabbaa, yurabbii)	sing	II, defective	ghannaa, yughannii	غ ن ي	غنّى ، يغنّي
45 (as khawwafa, yukhawwif)	change, alter	II, hollow	ghayyara, yughayyir	غ ى ر	غيّر ، يغير

⟵ ———— *Read this way*

Page reference	English	Verb Type	Transliteration	Root	Arabic verb
					ف
23–25 (as zaara, yazuur)	pass, go by	I, hollow	faata, yafuut	ف و ت	فات، يفوت
13–17	open	I, regular	fataHa, yaftaH	ف ت ح	فتح، يفتح
42–43 (as darrasa, yudarris)	search, inspect	II, regular	fattasha, yufattish	ف ت ش	فتّش، يفتّش
13–17	fail	I, regular	fashala, yafshal	ف ش ل	فشل، يفشل
42–43 (as darrasa, yudarris)	prefer	II, regular	faDDala, yufaDDil	ف ض ل	فضّل، يفضّل
13–17	have breakfast	I regular	faTara, yafTur	ف ط ر	فطر، يفطر
13–17	do	I, regular	faعala, yafعal	ف ع ل	فعل، يفعل
13–17	lose	I, regular	faqada, yafqid	ف ق د	فقد، يفقد
42–43 (as darrasa, yudarris)	think, reflect	II, regular	fakkara, yufakkir	ف ك ر	فكّر، يفكّر
13–17	understand	I, regular	fahima, yafham	ف ه م	فهم، يفهم
					ق
42–43 (as saabaqa, yusaabiq)	fight	III, regular	qaatala, yuqaatil	ق ت ل	قاتل، يقاتل
23–25 (as zaara, yazuur)	drive	I, hollow	qaada, yaquud	ق و د	قاد، يقود
23–25 (as Taara, yaTiir)	measure	I, hollow	qaasa, yaqiis	ق ي س	قاس، يقيس
23–25 (as zaara, yazuur)	say, tell	I, hollow	qaala, yaquul	ق و ل	قال، يقول
42–43 (as saabaqa, yusaabiq)	gamble	III, regular	qaamara, yuqaamir	ق م ر	قامر، يقامر
13–17	accept	I, regular	qabila, yaqbal	ق ب ل	قبل، يقبل
13–17	kill	I, regular	qatala, yaqtul	ق ت ل	قتل، يقتل
42–43 (as darrasa, yudarris)	massacre	II, regular	qattala, yuqattil	ق ت ل	قتّل، يقتّل
42–43 (as darrasa, yudarris)	estimate	II, regular	qaddara, yuqaddir	ق د ر	قدّر، يقدّر
42–43 (as darrasa, yudarris)	present, bring forward	II, regular	qaddama, yuqaddim	ق د م	قدّم، يقدّم
35–36	read	I, hamzated	qara'a, yaqra'	ق ر ء	قرأ، يقرأ
13–17	be/become near	I, regular	qaruba, yaqrub	ق ر ب	قرب، يقرب
13–17	bang	I, regular	qaraعa, yaqraع	ق ر ع	قرع، يقرع
42–43 (as darrasa, yudarris)	decide	II, regular	qarrara, yuqarrir	ق ر ر	قرّر، يقرّر
31 (as radda, yarudd)	cut	I, doubled	qaSSa, yaquSS	ق ص ص	قصّ، يقصّ
27–28 (as mashaa, yamshii)	judge	I, defective	qaDaa, yaqDii	ق ض ي	قضى، يقضي

Page reference	English	Verb Type	Transliteration	Root	Arabic verb
13–17	tear, cut	*I, regular*	qaTaعa, yaqTaع	ق ط ع	قطع، يقطع
13–17	jump	*I, regular*	qafaza, yaqfiz	ق ف ز	قفز، يقفز
13–17	shut, lock	*I, regular*	qafala, yaqfil	ق ف ل	قفل، يقفل
13–17	turn (something) over	*I, regular*	qalaba, yaqlib	ق ل ب	قلب، يقلب
27–28 (as mashaa, yamshii)	fry	*I, defective*	qalaa, yaqlii	ق ل ي	قلى، يقلي
					ك
23–25 (as naama, yanaam)	be about to	*I, hollow*	kaada, yakaad	ك و د	كاد، يكاد
45	reward	*III, hamzated*	kaafa'a, yukaafi'	ك ف ء	كافأ، يكافئ
23–25 (as zaara, yazuur)	be, exist	*I, hollow*	kaana, yakuun	ك و ن	كان، يكون
14–16	write	*I, regular*	kataba, yaktub	ك ت ب	كتب، يكتب
13–17	lie, tell lies	*I regular*	kadhaba, yakdhib	ك ذ ب	كذب، يكذب
13–17	hate	*I, regular*	kariha, yakrah	ك ر ه	كره، يكره
45 (as raddada, yuraddid)	repeat	*II, doubled*	karrara, yukarrir	ك ر ر	كرّر، يكرّر
13–17	win, earn	*I, regular*	kasaba, yaksib	ك س ب	كسب، يكسب
13–17	break	*I, regular*	kasara, yaksir	ك س ر	كسر، يكسر
42–43 (as darrasa, yudarris)	smash	*II, regular*	kassara, yukassir	ك س ر	كسّر، يكسّر
42–43 (as darrasa, yudarris)	cost	*II, regular*	kallafa, yukallif	ك ل ف	كلّف، يكلّف
13–17	sweep	*I, regular*	kanasa, yaknus	ك ن س	كنس، يكنس
27–28 (as mashaa, yamshii)	iron	*I, defective*	kawaa, yakwii	ك و ي	كوى، يكوي
					ل
45 (as saa'ala, yusaa'il)	be suitable	*III, hamzated*	laa'ama, yulaa'im	ل ء م	لاءم، يلائم
45	meet	*III, defective*	laaqaa, yulaaqii	ل ق ي	لاقى، يلاقي
13–17	wear	*I, regular*	labisa, yalbas	ل ب س	لبس، يلبس
13–17	play	*I, regular*	laعiba, yalعab	ل ع ب	لعب، يلعب
31 (as radda, yarudd)	turn	*I, doubled*	laffa, yaliff	ل ف ف	لفّ، يلفّ
27–28 (as nasiya, yansaa)	meet	*I, meet*	laqiya, yalqaa	ل ق ي	لقي، يلقى
13–17	touch	*I, regular*	lamasa, yalmis	ل م س	لمس، يلمس
45 (as khawwafa, yukhawwif)	pollute	*II, hollow*	lawwatha, yulawwith	ل و ث	لوّث، يلوّث
101	not to be	—	laysa	—	ليس

← *Read this way*

Page reference	English	Verb Type	Transliteration	Root	Arabic verb
					م
23–25 (as zaara, yazuur)	die	I, hollow	maata, yamuut	م و ت	مات، يموت
31 (as radda, yarudd)	extend, stretch	I, doubled	madda, yamudd	م د د	مدّ، يمدّ
31 (as radda, yarudd)	pass (by)	I, doubled	marra, yamurr	م ر ر	مرّ، يمرّ
13–17	wipe	I, regular	masaHa, yamsaH	م س ح	مسح، يمسح
13–17	hold, catch	I, regular	masaka, yamsik	م س ك	مسك، يمسك
27–28	walk	I, defective	mashaa, yamshii	م ش ي	مشى، يمشي
35–36 (as qara'a, yaqra')	fill	I, hamzated	mala'a, yamla'	م ل ء	ملأ، يملأ
13–17	own, possess	I, regular	malaka, yamlik	م ل ك	ملك، يملك
					ن
45 (as laaqaa, yulaaqii)	call out	III, defective	naadaa, yunaadii	ن د و	نادى، ينادي
42–43 (as saabaqa, yusaabiq)	discuss	III, regular	naaqasha, yunaaqish	ن ق ش	ناقش، يناقش
23–25	sleep	I, hollow	naama, yanaam	ن و م	نام، ينام
45	hand over	III, hollow	naawala, yunaawil	ن و ل	ناول، يناول
13–17	succeed	I, regular	najaHa, yanjaH	ن ج ح	نجح، ينجح
13–17	appoint, delegate	I, regular	nadaba, yandub	ن د ب	ندب، يندب
13–17	go down	I, regular	nazala, yanzil	ن ز ل	نزل، ينزل
27–28	forget	I, defective	nasiya, yansaa	ن س ي	نسي، ينسى
13–17	publish, diffuse	I, regular	nashara, yanshur	ن ش ر	نشر، ينشر
13–17	pronounce	I, regular	naTaqa, yanTuq	ن ط ق	نطق، ينطق
13–17	look	I, regular	naZara, yanZur	ن ظ ر	نظر، ينظر
42–43 (as darrasa, yudarris)	clean	II, regular	naZZafa, yunaZZif	ن ظ ف	نظّف، ينظّف
42–43 (as darrasa, yudarris)	organize	II, regular	naZZama, yunaZZim	ن ظ م	نظّم، ينظّم
13–17	transport	I, regular	naqala, yanqul	ن ق ل	نقل، ينقل
27–28 (as shakaa, yashkuu)	grow	I, defective	namaa, yanmuu	ن م و	نما، ينمو
27–28 (as mashaa, yamshii)	intend	I, defective	nawaa, yanwii	ن و ي	نوى، ينوي
					ه
42–43 (as saabaqa, yusaabiq)	emigrate	III, regular	haajara, yuhaajir	ه ج ر	هاجر، يهاجر

Page reference	English	Verb Type	Transliteration	Root	Arabic verb
13–17	land	*I, regular*	habaTa, yahbuT	ه ب ط	هبط، يهبط
13–17	escape	*I, regular*	haraba, yahrub	ه ر ب	هرب، يهرب
45	congratulate	*II, hamzated*	hanna', yuhanni'	ه ن ء	هنّأ، يهنّئ

و

45	agree	*III, assimilated*	waafaqa, yuwaafiq	و ف ق	وافق، يوافق
21–22 (as waSala, yaSil)	trust	*I, assimilated*	wathaqa, yathiq	و ث ق	وثق، يثق
21–22 (as waSala, yaSil)	find	*I, assimilated*	wajada, yajid	و ج د	وجد، يجد
31 (as radda, yarudd)	want, wish	*I, doubled*	wadda, yawadd	و د د	ودّ، يودّ
21–22 (as waSala, yaSil)	inherit	*I, assimilated*	waratha, yarith	و ر ث	ورث، يرث
45 (as waSSala, yuwaSSil)	distribute	*II, assimilated*	wazzaعa, yuwazziع	و ز ع	وزّع، يوزّع
21–22 (as waSala, yaSil)	describe	*I, assimilated*	waSafa, yaSif	و ص ف	وصف، يصف
21–22	arrive	*I, assimilated*	waSala, yaSil	و ص ل	وصل، يصل
45	deliver	*II, assimilated*	waSSala, yuwaSSil	و ص ل	وصّل، يوصّل
21–22 (as waSala, yaSil)	put, place	*I, assimilated*	waDaعa, yaDaع	و ض ع	وضع، يضع
45 (as waSSala, yuwaSSil)	employ	*II, assimilated*	waZZafa, yuwaZZif	و ظ ف	وظّف، يوظّف
45 (as waSSala, yuwaSSil)	save, economize	*II, assimilated*	waffara, yuwaffir	و ف ر	وفر، يوفّر
21–22 (as waSala, yaSil)	fall	*I, assimilated*	waqaعa, yaqaع	و ق ع	وقع، يقع
21–22 (as waSala, yaSil)	stand, stop	*I, assimilated*	waqafa, yaqif	و ق ف	وقف، يقف
27–28 (as mashaa, yamshii)	protect	*I, defective*	waqaa, yaqii	و ق ي	وقى، يقي
45 (as waSSala, yuwaSSil)	sign	*II, assimilated*	waqqaعa, yuwaqqiع	و ق ع	وقّع، يوقّع

ي

| 45 | facilitate | *II, assimilated* | yassara, yuyassir | ي س ر | يسّر، ييسّر |

Read this way ➛

English	Arabic verb	Root	Transliteration	Verb Type	Page Reference
A					
abandon	ترك، يترك	ت ر ك	taraka, yatruk	*I, regular*	13–17
able (be)	استطاع، يستطيع	ط و ع	istaTaaعa, yastaTiiع	*X, hollow*	(as istaqaala, yastaqiil) 60
accept	قبل، يقبل	ق ب ل	qabila, yaqbal	*I, regular*	13–17
accustomed (be)	اعتاد، يعتاد	ع و د	iعtaada, yaعtaad	*VIII, hollow*	(as iHtaaja, yaHtaaj) 60
add	أضاف، يضيف	ض ي ف	'aDaafa, yuDiif	*IV, hollow*	(as 'araada, yuriid) 45
adjust	عدّل، يعدّل	ع د ل	عaddala, yuعaddil	*II, regular*	(as darrasa, yudarris) 42–43
admire	استحسن، يستحسن	ح س ن	istaHsana, yastaHsin	*X, regular*	(as istaعlama, yastaعlim) 57–58
adopt (measures, etc.)	اتّخذ، يتّخذ	ء خ ذ	ittakhadha, yattakhidh	*VIII, hamzated*	60
advance	اقترب، يقترب	ق ر ب	iqtaraba, yaqtarib	*VIII, regular*	57–58
agree	اتّفق، يتّفق	و ق ف	ittafaqa, yattafiq	*VIII, assimilated*	60
	وافق، يوافق	و ف ق	waafaqa, yuwaafiq	*III, assimilated*	45
agree together	توافق، يتوافق	و ف ق	tawaafaqa, yatawaafaq	*VI, assimilated*	52
allow	سمح، يسمح	س م ح	samuHa, yasmuH	*I, regular*	13–17
amused (be)	تسلّى، يتسلّى	س ل و	tasallaa, yatasallaa	*V, defective*	(as tamannaa, yatamannaa) 52
annoyed (be)	تضايق، يتضايق	ض ي ق	taDaayaqa, yataDaayaq	*VI, hollow*	(as taعaawana, yataعaawan) 52
answer	ردّ، يردّ	ر د د	radda, yarudd	*I, doubled*	31
	أجاب، يجيب	ج و ب	'ajaaba, yajiib	*IV, hollow*	(as 'araada, yuriid) 45
apologize	اعتذر، يعتذر	ع ذ ر	iعtadhara, yaعtadhir	*VIII, regular*	(as iqtaraba, yaqtarib) 57–58
appear	بدا، يبدو	ب د و	badaa, yabduu	*I, defective*	(as shakaa, yashkuu) 27–28
	ظهر، يظهر	ظ ه ر	Zahara, yaZhar	*I, regular*	13–17
appoint	ندب، يندب	ن د ب	nadaba, yandub	*I, regular*	13–17
approach	اقترب، يقترب	ق ر ب	iqtaraba, yaqtarib	*VIII, regular*	57–58
approve	رضي، يرضى	ر ض ي	raDiya, yarDaa	*I, defective*	(as nasiya, yansaa) 27–28
argue	جادل، يجادل	ج د ل	jaadala, yajaadil	*III, regular*	(as saabaqa, yusaabiq) 42–43
arrange	رتّب، يرتّب	ر ت ب	rattaba, yurattib	*II, regular*	(as darrasa, yudarris) 42–43
arrive	وصل، يصل	و ص ل	waSala, yaSil	*I, assimilated*	21–22
ask	سأل، يسأل	س ء ل	sa'ala, yas'al	*I, hamzated*	35–36
ask for permission	استأذن، يستأذن	ء ذ ن	ista'dhana, yasta'dhin	*X, hamzated*	(as ista'jara, yasta'jir) 60

Read this way ──────➤

English	Arabic verb	Root	Transliteration	Verb Type	Page Reference
attempt	سعي، يسعى	س ع ي	saɛiya, yasɛaa	I, defective	(as nasiya, yansaa) 27–28
attend	حضر، يحضر	ح ض ر	HaDara, yaHDur	I, regular	13–17
attention: pay attention	انتبه، ينتبه	ن ب ه	intabaha, yantabih	VIII, regular	(as iqtaraba, yaqtarib) 57–58

B

bang	قرع، يقرع	ق ر ع	qaraɛa, yaqraɛ	I, regular	13–17
bathe	استحمّ، يستحمّ	ح م م	istaHamma, yastaHimm	X, doubled	(as istamarra, yastamirr) 60
be	كان، يكون	ك و ن	kaana, yakuun	I, hollow	(as zaara, yazuur) 23–25
be: not to be	ليس	—	laysa	—	101
be about to	كاد، يكاد	ك و د	kaada, yakaad	I, hollow	(as naama, yanaam) 23–25
beautiful (be)	حسن، يحسن	ح س ن	Hasana, yaHsun	I, regular	13–17
become	صار، يصير	ص ي ر	Saara, yaSiir	I, hollow	(as Taara, yaTiir) 23–25
	أصبح، يصبح	ص ب ح	ʼaSbaHa, yuSbiH	IV, regular	(as ʼaɛlama, yuɛlim) 42–43
begin	بدأ، يبدأ	ب د ء	badaʼa, yabdaʼ	I, hamzated	(as qaraʼa, yaqraʼ) 35–36
	ابتدأ، يبتدئ	ب د ء	ibtadaʼa, yabtadiʼ	VIII, hamzated	60
behave	تصرّف، يتصرّف	ص ر ف	taSarrafa, yataSarraf	V, regular (as tadhakkara, yatadhakkar) 49–50
believe	اعتقد، يعتقد	ع ق د	iɛtaqada, yaɛtaqid	VIII, regular	(as iqtaraba, yaqtarib) 57–58
	صدّق، يصدّق	ص د ق	Saddaqa, yuSSadiq	II, regular	(as darrasa, yudarris) 42–43
believe in	آمن، يؤمن	ء م ن	ʼaamana, yuʼmin	IV, hamzated	45
benefit	أفاد، يفيد	ف ي د	ʼafaada, yufiid	IV, hollow	(as ʼaraada, yuriid) 45
betray	خان، يخون	خ و ن	khaana, yakhuun	I, hollow	(as zaara, yazuur) 23–25
blame	آخذ، يؤاخذ	ء خ ذ	ʼaakhadha, yuʼaakhidh	III, hamzated	45
block	سدّ، يسدّ	س د د	sadda, yasudd	I, doubled	(as radda, yarudd) 31
boil	غلى، يغلي	غ ل ي	ghalaa, yaghlii	I, defective	(as mashaa, yamshii) 27–28
bore (someone)	أسأم، يسئم	س ء م	ʼasʼama, yuʼsim	IV, hamzated	45
borrow	اقترض، يقترض	ق ر ض	iqtaraDa, yaqtariD	VIII, regular	(as darrasa, yudarris) 42–43
bow	انحنى، ينحني	ن ح و	inHanaa, yanHanii	VII, defective	60
break	كسر، يكسر	ك س ر	kasara, yaksir	I, regular	13–17
breakfast (have)	فطر، يفطر	ف ط ر	faTara, yafTur	I regular	13–17
breed	ربّى، يربّي	ر ب و	rabbaa, yurabbii	II, defective	45

Read this way ⟶

English	Arabic verb	Root	Transliteration	Verb Type	Page Reference
broken (be)	انكسر، ينكسر	ك س ر	inkasara, yankasir	*VII, regular*	(as inqalaba, yanqalib) 57–58
build	بنى، يبني	ب ن ي	banaa, yabnii	*I, defective*	(as mashaa, yamshii) 27–28
burn	حرق، يحرق	ح ر ق	Haraqa, yaHriq	*I, regular*	13–17
buy	اشترى، يشتري	ش ر ي	ishtaraa, yashtarii	*VIII, defective*	60

C

call out	نادى، ينادي	ن د و	naadaa, yunaadii	*III, defective*	(as laaqaa, yulaaqii) 45
capsize	انقلب، ينقلب	ق ل ب	inqalaba, yanqalib	*VII, regular*	57–58
carry	حمل، يحمل	ح م ل	Hamala, yaHmil	*I, regular*	13–17
catch	مسك، يمسك	م س ك	masaka, yamsik	*I, regular*	13–17
cause	سبّب، يسبّب	س ب ب	sabbaba, yusabbib	*II, doubled*	(as raddada, yuraddid) 45
celebrate	احتفل، يحتفل	ح ف ل	iHtafala, yaHtafil	*VIII, regular*	(as iqtaraba, yaqtarib) 57–58
change (alter)	غيّر، يغيّر	غ ي ر	ghayyara, yughayyir	*II, hollow*	(as khawwafa, yukhawwif) 45
change (money)	صرّف، يصرّف	ص ر ف	Sarrafa, yuSarrif	*II, regular*	(as darrasa, yudarris) 42–43
charge (battery)	شحن، يشحن	ش ح ن	'ahamma, yuhimm	*I, regular*	13–17
chatter	ثرثر، يثرثر	ث ر ث ر	tharthara, yutharthir	*I, quadriliteral*	97
choose	اختار، يختار	خ ي ر	ikhtaara, yakhtaar	*VIII, hollow*	(as iHtaaja, yaHtaaj) 60
clean	نظّف، ينظّف	ن ظ ف	naZZafa, yunaZZif	*II, regular*	(as darrasa, yudarris) 42–43
climb	تسلّق، يتسلّق	س ل ق	tasallaqa, yatasallaq	*V, regular*	(as tadhakkara, yatadhakkar) 49–50
coach	درّب، يدرّب	د ر ب	darraba, yudarrib	*II, regular*	(as darrasa, yudarris) 42–43
cold: be/go cold	برد، يبرد	ب ر د	barada, yabrad	*I, regular*	13–17
collect	جمع، يجمع	ج م ع	jamaعa, yajmaع	*I, regular*	13–17
colored (be)	تلوّن، يتلوّن	ل و ن	talawwana, yatalawwan	*V, hollow*	52
come	جاء، يجيء	ج ي ء	jaa'a, yajii'	*I, hollow, hamzated*	99
	أتى، يأتي	ء ت ي	'ataa, ya'tii	*I, defective, hamzated*	(as mashaa, yamshii) 27–28
command	أمر، يأمر	ء م ر	'amara, ya'mur	*I, hamzated*	(as 'akhadha, ya'khudh) 35-36
complain	شكا، يشكو	ش ك و	shakaa, yashkuu	*I, defective*	27–28
confirm	أكّد، يؤكّد	ء ك د	'akkada, yu'akkid	*II, hamzated*	(as 'aththara, yu'aththir) 45
congratulate	هنّأ، يهنّئ	ه ن ء	hanna', yuhanni'	*II, hamzated*	45
connect	أوصل، يوصل	و ص ل	'awSala, yuuSil	*IV, assimilated*	45

Read this way ———————➤

English	Arabic verb	Root	Transliteration	Verb Type	Page Reference
construct	أنشأ، ينشئ	ن ش ء	'ansha'a, yunshi'	IV, hamzated	45
contact	اتّصل، يتّصل	و ص ل	ittaSala, yattaSil	VIII, assimilated	(as ittafaqa, yattafiq) 60
contain	احتوى، يحتوي	ح و ي	iHtawaa, yaHtawii	VIII, defective	(as ishtaraa, yashtarii) 60
continue	استمرّ، يستمرّ	م ر ر	istamarra, yastamirr	X, doubled	60
converse	تحادث، يتحادث	ح د ث	taHaadatha, yataHaadath	VI, regular	49–50
cook	طبخ، يطبخ	ط ب خ	Tabakha, yaTbukh	I, regular	13–17
cooperate	تعاون، يتعاون	ع و ن	taعaawana, yataعaawan	VI, hollow	52
cost	كلّف، يكلّف	ك ل ف	kallafa, yukallif	II, regular	(as darrasa, yudarris) 42–43
cough	سعل، يسعل	س ع ل	saعala, yasعul	I, regular	13–17
count	عدّ، يعدّ	ع د د	عadda, yaعudd	I, doubled	(as radda, yarudd) 31
cover	غطّى، يغطّي	غ ط و	ghaTTaa, yughaTTii	II, defective	(as rabbaa, yurabbii) 45
crackle	طقطق، يطقطق	ط ق ط ق	TaqTaqa, yuTaqTiq	I, quadriliteral	(daHraja, yudaHrij) 97
cross (road, etc.)	عبر، يعبر	ع ب ر	عabara, yaعbur	I, regular	13–17
crowd	ازدحم، يزدحم	ز ح م	izdaHama, yazdaHim	VIII, irregular	55
cut	قصّ، يقصّ	ق ص ص	qaSSa, yaquSS	I, doubled	(as radda, yarudd) 31
	قطع، يقطع	ق ط ع	qaTaعa, yaqTaع	I, regular	13–17

D

dance	رقص، يرقص	ر ق ص	raqaSa, yarquS	I, regular	13–17
deal with	عامل، يعامل	ع م ل	عaamala, yuعaamil	III, regular	(as saabaqa, yusaabiq) 42–43
decide	قرّر، يقرّر	ق ر ر	qarrara, yuqarrir	II, regular	(as darrasa, yudarris) 42–43
delegate	ندب، يندب	ن د ب	nadaba, yandub	I, regular	13–17
deliver	وصّل، يوصّل	و ص ل	waSSala, yuwaSSil	II, assimilated	45
depart	غادر، يغادر	غ د ر	ghaadara, yughaadir	III, regular	(as saabaqa, yusaabiq) 42–43
	انصرف، ينصرف	ص ر ف	inSarafa, yanSarif	VII, regular	(as inqalaba, yanqalib) 57–58
deposit	أودع، يودع	و د ع	'awdaعa, yuudiع	IV, assimilated	(as 'awSala, yuuSil) 45
describe	وصف، يصف	و ص ف	waSafa, yaSif	I, assimilated	(as waSala, yaSil) 21–22
deserve	استحقّ، يستحقّ	ح ق ق	istaHaqqa, yastaHiqq	X, doubled	(as istamarra, yastamirr) 60
determine	قدّر، يقدّر	ق د ر	qaddara, yuqaddir	II, regular	(as darrasa, yudarris) 42–43
die	مات، يموت	م و ت	maata, yamuut	I, hollow	(as zaara, yazuur) 23–25

Read this way ——————→

English	Arabic verb	Root	Transliteration	Verb Type	Page Reference
differentiated (be)	امتاز، يمتاز	م ي ز	imtaaza, yamtaaz	*VIII, hollow*	(as iHtaaja, yaHtaaj) 60
dine (have dinner)	تعشّى، يتعشّى	ع ش ي	taعashshaa, yataعashshaa	*V, defective*	(as tamannaa, yatamannaa) 52
discuss	ناقش، يناقش	ن ق ش	naaqasha, yunaaqish	*III, regular*	(as saabaqa, yusaabiq) 42–43
dispersed (be)	تفارق، يتفارق	ف ر ق	tafaaraqa, yatafaaraq	*VI, regular*	(as taHaadatha, yataHaadath) 49–50
distribute	وزّع، يوزّع	و ز ع	wazzaعa, yuwazziع	*II, assimilated*	(as waSSala, yuwaSSil) 45
disturbed (be)	اضطرب، يضطرب	ض ر ب	iDTaraba, yaDTarib	*VIII, irregular*	55–56
divided (be)	انقسم، ينقسم	ق س م	inqasama, yanqasim	*VII, regular*	(as inqalaba, yanqalib) 57–58
do	عمل، يعمل	ع م ل	عamila, yaعmal	*I, regular*	13–17
	فعل، يفعل	ف ع ل	faعala, yafعal	*I, regular*	13–17
doubt	شكّ، يشكّ	ش ك ك	shakka, yashukk	*I, doubled*	(as radda, yarudd) 31
download	حمّل، يحمّل	ح م ل	Hammala, yuHammil	*II, regular*	(as darrasa, yudarris) 42–43
draw (a picture)	رسم، يرسم	ر س م	rasama, yarsum	*I, regular*	13–17
drink	شرب، يشرب	ش ر ب	shariba, yashrab	*I, regular*	13–17
drive	قاد، يقود	ق و د	qaada, yaquud	*I, hollow*	(as zaara, yazuur) 23–25

E

English	Arabic verb	Root	Transliteration	Verb Type	Page Reference
earn	كسب، يكسب	ك س ب	kasaba, yaksib	*I, regular*	13–17
eat	أكل، يأكل	ء ك ل	'akala, ya'kul	*I, hamzated*	(as 'akhadha, ya'khudh) 35-36
emigrate	هاجر، يهاجر	ه ج ر	haajara, yuhaajir	*III, regular*	(as saabaqa, yusaabiq) 42–43
employ	وظّف، يوظّف	و ظ ف	waZZafa, yuwaZZif	*II, assimilated*	(as waSSala, yuwaSSil) 45
enjoy	استمتع، يستمتع	م ت ع	istamtaعa, yastamtiع	*X, regular*	(as istaعlama, yastaعlim) 57–58
enquire	استعلم، يستعلم	ع ل م	istaعlama, yastaعlim	*X, regular*	57–58
enroll	انضمّ، ينضمّ	ض م م	inDamma, yanDamm	*VII, doubled*	60
enter	دخل، يدخل	د خ ل	dakhala, yadkhul	*I, regular*	13–17
equal	ساوى، يساوي	س و ي	saawaa, yusaawii	*III, defective*	(as laaqaa, yulaaqii) 45
equal (be)	تكافأ، يتكافأ	ك ف ء	takaafa'a, yatakaafa'	*VI, hamzated*	52
escape	هرب، يهرب	ه ر ب	haraba, yahrub	*I, regular*	13–17
establish	أسّس، يؤسّس	ء س س	'assasa, yu'assis	*II, doubled, hamzated*	(as 'aththara, yu'aththir) 45
estimate	قدّر، يقدّر	ق د ر	qaddara, yuqaddir	*II, regular*	(as darrasa, yudarris) 42–43
examine	امتحن، يمتحن	م ح ن	imtaHana, yamtaHin	*VIII, regular*	(as iqtaraba, yaqtarib) 57–58

Read this way ──────────➤

English	Arabic verb	Root	Transliteration	Verb Type	Page Reference
excel	تفوّق، يتفوّق	ف و ق	tafawwaqa, yatafawwaq	V, regular (as tadhakkara, yatadhakkar)	49–50
exclude	استثنى، يستثني	ث ن ي	istathnaa, yastathnii	X, defective	60
exist	كان، يكون	ك و ن	kaana, yakuun	I, hollow (as zaara, yazuur)	23–25
exit	خرج، يخرج	خ ر ج	kharaja, yakhruj	I, regular	13–17
expect	توقّع، يتوقّع	و ق ع	tawaqqaعa, yatawaqqaع	V, assimilated	52
explore	استكشف، يستكشف	ك ش ف	istakshafa, yastakshif	X, regular (as istaعlama, yastaعlim)	57–58
extend	امتدّ، يمتدّ	م د د	imtadda, yamtadd	VIII, doubled	60
	مدّ، يمدّ	م د د	madda, yamudd	I, doubled (as radda, yarudd)	31
extinguish	أطفأ، يطفئ	ط ف ء	'aTfa'a, yuTfi'	IV, hamzated (as 'ansha'a, yunshi')	45
extract	استخرج، يستخرج	خ ر ج	istakhraja, yastakhrij	X, regular (as istaعlama, yastaعlim)	57–58

F

English	Arabic verb	Root	Transliteration	Verb Type	Page Reference
facilitate	يسّر، ييسّر	ي س ر	yassara, yuyassir	II, assimilated	45
fail	فشل، يفشل	ف ش ل	fashala, yafshal	I, regular	13–17
fall	سقط، يسقط	س ق ط	saqaTa, yasquT	I, regular	13–17
	وقع، يقع	و ق ع	waqaعa, yaqaع	I, assimilated (as waSala, yaSil)	21–22
familiar (be)	تآلف، يتآلف	ء ل ف	ta'aalafa, yata'aalaf	VI, hamzated	52
fast	صام، يصوم	ص و م	Saama, yaSuum	I, hollow (as zaara, yazuur)	23–25
fear	خاف، يخاف	خ و ف	khaafa, yakhaaf	I, hollow (as naama, yanaam)	23–25
fed up (be)	سئم، يسأم	س ء م	sa'ima, yas'am	I, hamzated (as sa'ala, yas'al)	35–36
feel	شعر، يشعر	ش ع ر	shaعara, yashعur	I, regular	13–17
fight	قاتل، يقاتل	ق ت ل	qaatala, yuqaatil	III, regular (as saabaqa, yusaabiq)	42–43
fill	ملأ، يملأ	م ل ء	mala'a, yamla'	I, hamzated (as qara'a, yaqra')	35–36
find	وجد، يجد	و ج د	wajada, yajid	I, assimilated (as waSala, yaSil)	21–22
finish	أنهى، ينهي	ن ه ء	'anhaa, yunhii	IV, defective (as 'aعTaa, yuعTii)	45
	انتهى، ينتهي	ن ه ي	intahaa, yantahii	VIII, defective (as ishtaraa, yashtarii)	60
finished (be)	انقضى، ينقضي	ق ض ي	inqaDaa, yanqaDii	VII, defective (as inHanaa, yanHanii)	60
	تمّ، يتمّ	ت م م	tamma, yatimm	I, doubled (as radda, yarudd)	31
fly	طار، يطير	ط ي ر	Taara, yaTiir	I, hollow	23–25
follow	تبع، يتبع	ت ب ع	tabaعa, yatbaع	I, regular	13–17

English	Arabic verb	Root	Transliteration	Verb Type	Page Reference
follow one another	سلسل، يتسلسل تسلسل	س ل س ل	tasalsala, yatasalsal	II, quadriliteral	(as tafalsafa, yatafalsaf) 98
forget	نسي، ينسى	ن س ي	nasiya, yansaa	I, defective	27–28
found	أنشأ، ينشئ	ن ش ء	'ansha'a, yunshi'	IV, hamzated	45
	أسّس، يؤسّس	ء س س	'assasa, yu'assis	II, doubled, hamzated	(as 'aththara, yu'aththir) 45
frighten	خوّف، يخوّف	خ و ف	khawwafa, yukhawwif	II, hollow	45
fry	قلى، يقلي	ق ل ي	qalaa, yaqlii	I, defective	(as mashaa, yamshii) 27–28

G

gamble	قامر، يقامر	ق م ر	qaamara, yuqaamir	III, regular	(as saabaqa, yusaabiq) 42–43
gargle	غرغر، يغرغر	غ ر غ ر	gharghara, yugharghir	I, quadriliteral	97
get on	ركب، يركب	ر ك ب	rakiba, yarkab	I, regular	13–17
give	أعطى، يعطي	ع ط و	'aعTaa, yuعTii	IV, defective	45
go	ذهب، يذهب	ذ ه ب	dhahaba, yadh-hab	I, regular	13–17
go down	نزل، ينزل	ن ز ل	nazala, yanzil	I, regular	13–17
go out	خرج، يخرج	خ ر ج	kharaja, yakhruj	I, regular	13–17
grow	نما، ينمو	ن م و	namaa, yanmuu	I, defective	(as shakaa, yashkuu) 27–28

H

hand over	ناول، يناول	ن و ل	naawala, yunaawil	III, hollow	45
happen	حدث، يحدث	ح د ث	Hadatha, yaHduth	I, regular	13–17
hate	كره، يكره	ك ر ه	kariha, yakrah	I, regular	13–17
hear	سمع، يسمع	س م ع	samiعa, yasmaع	I, regular	13–17
heat	سخّن، يسخّن	س خ ن	sakhkhana, yusakhkhin	II, regular	(as darrasa, yudarris) 42–43
help	عاون، يعاون	ع و ن	عaawana, yuعaawin	III, hollow	(as naawala, yunaawil) 45
	ساعد، يساعد	س ع د	saaعada, yusaaعid	III, regular	(as saabaqa, yusaabiq) 42–43
hesitate	تردّد، يتردّد	ر د د	taraddada, yataraddad	V, doubled	52
hire	استأجر، يستأجر	ء ج ر	ista'jara, yasta'jir	X, hamzated	60
	أجّر، يؤجّر	ء ج ر	'ajjara, yu'ajjir	II, hamzated	(as 'aththara, yu'aththir) 45
hit	ضرب، يضرب	ض ر ب	Daraba, yaDrub	I, regular	13–17
hold	مسك، يمسك	م س ك	masaka, yamsik	I, regular	13–17

Read this way ──────►

English	Arabic verb	Root	Transliteration	Verb Type	Page Reference
hope	رجا، يرجو	ر ج و	rajaa, yarjuu	I, defective	(as shakaa, yashkuu) 27–28
	أمل، يأمل	ء م ل	'amala, ya'mul	I, hamzated	(as 'akhadha, ya'khudh) 35–36
hot (be)	سخن، يسخن	س خ ن	sakhana, yaskhun	I, regular	13–17
hum	دندن، يدندن	د ن د ن	dandana, yudandin	I, quadriliteral	97
hurry	أسرع، يسرع	س ر ع	'asraعa, yusriع	IV, regular	(as 'aعlama, yuعlim) 42–43
hurt	آلم، يؤلم	ء ل م	'aalama, yu'lim	IV, hamzated	(as 'aamana, yu'min) 45

I

imagine	تصوّر، يتصوّر	ص و ر	taSawwara, yataSawwar	V, hollow	(as talawwana, yatalawwan) 52
import	استورد، يستورد	و ر د	istawrada, yastawrid	X, assimilated	(as istawqafa, yastawqif) 60
improve	تحسّن، يتحسّن	ح س ن	taHassana, yataHassan	V, regular	(as tadhakkara, yatadhakkar) 49–50
	حسّن، يحسّن	ح س ن	Hassana, yuHassin	II, regular	(as darrasa, yudarris) 42–43
increase	زاد، يزيد	ز ي د	zaada, yaziid	I, hollow	(as Taara, yaTiir) 23–25
indicate	دلّ، يدلّ	د ل ل	dalla, yadull	I, doubled	(as radda, yarudd) 31
	أشار، يشير	ش و ر	'ashaara, yushiir	IV, hollow	(as 'araada, yuriid) 45
influence	أثّر، يؤثّر	ء ث ر	'aththara, yu'aththir	II, hamzated	45
influenced (be)	تأثّر، يتأثّر	ء ث ر	ta'aththara, yata'aththar	V, hamzated	52
inform	أعلم، يعلم	ع ل م	'aعlama, yuعlim	IV, regular	42–43
	أخبر، يخبر	خ ب ر	'akhbara, yukhbir	IV, regular	(as 'aعlama, yuعlim) 42–43
informed about (be)	اطّلع، يطّلع	ط ل ع	iTTalaعa, yaTTaliع	VIII, irregular	55–56
inherit	ورث، يرث	و ر ث	waratha, yarith	I, assimilated	(as waSala, yaSil) 21–22
insist	أصرّ، يصرّ	ص ر ر	'aSarra, yuSirr	IV, doubled	(as 'aHabba, yuHibb) 45
inspect	فتّش، يفتّش	ف ت ش	fattasha, yufattish	II, regular	(as darrasa, yudarris) 42–43
intend	نوى، ينوي	ن و ي	nawaa, yanwii	I, defective	(as mashaa, yamshii) 27–28
invite	دعا، يدعو	د ع و	daعaa, yadعuu	I, defective	(as shakaa, yashkuu) 27–28
iron	كوى، يكوي	ك و ي	kawaa, yakwii	I, defective	(as mashaa, yamshii) 27–28

J

jail	سجن، يسجن	س ج ن	sajana, yasjun	I, regular	13–17
join	انضمّ، ينضمّ	ض م م	inDamma, yanDamm	VII, doubled	60
judge	قضى، يقضي	ق ض ي	qaDaa, yaqDii	I, defective	(as mashaa, yamshii) 27–28

Read this way ⟶

English	Arabic verb	Root	Transliteration	Verb Type	Page Reference
jump	قفز، يقفز	ق ف ز	qafaza, yaqfiz	I, regular	13–17

K

kill	قتل، يقتل	ق ت ل	qatala, yaqtul	I, regular	13–17
knock (on door, etc.)	طرق، يطرق	ط ر ق	Taraqa, yaTruq	I, regular	13–17
know	علم، يعلم	ع ل م	εalima, yaεlam	I, regular	13–17
	عرف، يعرف	ع ر ف	εarafa, yaεrif	I, regular	13–17

L

land	هبط، يهبط	ه ب ط	habaTa, yahbuT	I, regular	13–17
last	دام، يدوم	د و م	daama, yaduum	I, hollow	(as zaara, yazuur) 23–25
late (be)	تأخّر، يتأخّر	ء خ ر	ta'akhkhara, yata'akhkhar	V, hamzated	(as ta'aththara, yata'aththar) 52
laugh	ضحك، يضحك	ض ح ك	DaHika, yaDHak	I, regular	13–17
lazy (be)	تكاسل، يتكاسل	ك س ل	takaasala, yatakaasal	VI, regular (as taHaadatha, yataHaadath) 49–50
learn	تعلّم، يتعلّم	ع ل م	taεallama, yataεallam	V, regular (as tadhakkara, yatadhakkar) 49–50
leave (abandon)	ترك، يترك	ت ر ك	taraka, yatruk	I, regular	13–17
led (be)	انقاد، ينقاد	ق و د	inqaada, yanqaad	VII, hollow	60
lend	أعار، يعير	ع و ر	'aεaara, yuεiir	IV, hollow	(as 'araada, yuriid) 45
liberate	أطلق، يطلق	ط ل ق	'aTlaqa, yaTliq	IV, regular	(as 'aεlama, yuεlim) 42–43
lie (tell lies)	كذب، يكذب	ك ذ ب	kadhaba, yakdhib	I regular	13–17
lift up	رفع، يرفع	ر ف ع	rafaεa, yarfaε	I, regular	13–17
like	أحبّ، يحبّ	ح ب ب	'aHabba, yuHibb	IV, doubled	45
listen	استمع، يستمع	س م ع	istamaεa, yastamiε	VIII, regular (as iqtaraba, yaqtarib) 57–58
live	عاش، يعيش	ع ي ش	εaasha, yaεiish	I, hollow	(as Taara, yaTiir) 23–25
	سكن، يسكن	س ك ن	sakana, yaskun	I, regular	13–17
lock	قفل، يقفل	ق ف ل	qafala, yaqfil	I, regular	13–17
look	نظر، ينظر	ن ظ ر	naZara, yanZur	I, regular	13–17
lose	فقد، يفقد	ف ق د	faqada, yafqid	I, regular	13–17
lost: be/get lost	تاه، يتوه	ت و ه	taaha, yatuuh	I, hollow	(as zaara, yazuur) 23–25
love	أحبّ، يحبّ	ح ب ب	'aHabba, yuHibb	IV, doubled	45
lunch (have)	تغدّى، يتغدّى	غ د و	taghaddaa, yataghaddaa	V, defective	(as tamannaa, yatamannaa) 52

Read this way ⟶

English	Arabic verb	Root	Transliteration	Verb Type	Page Reference
M					
make	صنع، يصنع	ص ن ع	Sanaعa, yaSnaع	I, regular	13–17
manage (e.g. business)	أدار، يدير	د و ر	'adaara, yudiir	IV, hollow	(as 'araada, yuriid) 45
manufacture	صنع، يصنع	ص ن ع	Sanaعa, yaSnaع	I, regular	13–17
marry	تزوّج، يتزوّج	ز و ج	tazawwaja, yatazawwaj	V, hollow	(as talawwana, yatalawwan) 52
massacre	قتّل، يقتّل	ق ت ل	qattala, yuqattil	II, regular	(as darrasa, yudarris) 42–43
measure	قاس، يقيس	ق ي س	qaasa, yaqiis	I, hollow	(as Taara, yaTiir) 23–25
meet	اجتمع، يجتمع	ج م ع	ijtamaعa, yajtamiع	VIII, regular	(as iqtaraba, yaqtarib) 57–58
	لاقى، يلاقي	ل ق ي	laaqaa, yulaaqii	III, defective	45
	لقي، يلقى	ل ق ي	laqiya, yalqaa	I, meet	(as nasiya, yansaa) 27–28
meet up	تلاقى، يتلاقى	ل ق ي	talaaqaa, yatalaaqaa	VI, defective	52
memorize, save to memory	حفظ، يحفظ	ح ف ظ	HafiZa, yaHfaZ	I, regular	13–17
mention	ذكر، يذكر	ذ ك ر	dhakara, yadhkur	I, regular	13–17
mock	استهزأ، يستهزئ	ه ز ء	istahza'a, yastahzi'	X, hamzated	60
move	تحرّك، يتحرّك	ح ر ك	taHarraka, yataHarrak	V, regular	(as tadhakkara, yatadhakkar) 49–50
	حرّك، يحرّك	ح ر ك	Harraka, yuHarrik	II, regular	(as darrasa, yudarris) 42–43
mutter	تمتم، يتمتم	ت م ت م	tamtama, yutamtim	I, quadriliteral	97
N					
name	سمّى، يسمّي	س م ي	sammaa, yusammii	II, defective	(as rabbaa, yurabbii) 45
near (be/become)	قرب، يقرب	ق ر ب	qaruba, yaqrub	I, regular	13–17
need	احتاج، يحتاج	ح و ج	iHtaaja, yaHtaaj	VIII, hollow	60
O					
occupy (land, etc.)	احتلّ، يحتلّ	ح ل ل	iHtalla, yaHtall	VIII, doubled	(as imtadda, yamtadd) 60
open	فتح، يفتح	ف ت ح	fataHa, yaftaH	I, regular	13–17
oppose	ضادّ، يضادّ	ض د د	Daadd, yuDaadd	III, doubled	45
optimistic (be)	تفأل، يتفأل	ف ء ل	tafa''ala, yatafa''al	V, hamzated	52
organize	نظّم، ينظّم	ن ظ م	naZZama, yunaZZim	II, regular	(as darrasa, yudarris) 42–43
own	ملك، يملك	م ل ك	malaka, yamlik	I, regular	13–17

Read this way ➞

English	Arabic verb	Root	Transliteration	Verb Type	Page Reference
P					
participate	اشترك، يشترك	ش ر ك	ishtaraka, yashtarik	VIII, regular (as iqtaraba, yaqtarib) 57–58
pass (by)	مرّ، يمرّ	م ر ر	marra, yamurr	I, doubled (as radda, yarudd) 31
pass, go by	فات، يفوت	ف و ت	faata, yafuut	I, hollow (as zaara, yazuur) 23–25
pay	دفع، يدفع	د ف ع	dafaعa, yadfaع	I, regular 13–17
perfume (put on)	تعطّر، يتعطّر	ع ط ر	taعaTTara, yataعaTTar	V, regular (as tadhakkara, yatadhakkar) 49–50
permit	أذن، يأذن	ء ذ ن	'adhina, ya'dhan	I, hamzated (as 'akhadha, ya'khudh) 35–36
philosophize	تفلسف، يتفلسف	ف ل س ف	tafalsafa, yatafalsaf	II, quadriliteral 98
place	وضع، يضع	و ض ع	waDaعa, yaDaع	I, assimilated (as waSala, yaSil) 21–22
plant	زرع، يزرع	ز ر ع	zaraعa, yazraع	I, regular 13–17
play	لعب، يلعب	ل ع ب	laعiba, yalعab	I, regular 13–17
play (an instrument)	عزف، يعزف	ع ز ف	عazafa, yaعzif	I, regular 13–17
pollute	لوّث، يلوّث	ل و ث	lawwatha, yulawwith	II, hollow (as khawwafa, yukhawwif) 45
polluted (be)	تلوّث، يتلوّث	ل و ث	talawwatha, yatalawwath	V, regular (as tadhakkara, yatadhakkar) 49–50
possess	ملك، يملك	م ل ك	malaka, yamlik	I, regular 13–17
pray	صلّى، يصلّي	ص ل و	Sallaa, yuSallii	II, defective (as rabbaa, yurabbii) 45
precede	سبق، يسبق	س ب ق	sabaqa, yasbiq	I, regular 13–17
predict	تنبّأ، يتنبّأ	ن ب ء	tanabba'a, yatanabba'	V, hamzated 52
prefer	فضّل، يفضّل	ف ض ل	faDDala, yufaDDil	II, regular (as darrasa, yudarris) 42–43
prepare	جهّز، يجهّز	ج ه ز	jahhaza, yujahhiz	II, regular (as darrasa, yudarris) 42–43
	أعدّ، يعدّ	ع د د	'aعadda, yuعidd	IV, doubled (as 'aHabba, yuHibb) 45
present	قدّم، يقدّم	ق د م	qaddama, yuqaddim	II, regular (as darrasa, yudarris) 42–43
print	طبع، يطبع	ط ب ع	Tabaعa, yaTbaع	I, regular 13–17
pronounce	نطق، ينطق	ن ط ق	naTaqa, yanTuq	I, regular 13–17
protect	حمى، يحمي	ح م ي	Hamaa, yaHmii	I, defective (as mashaa, yamshii) 27–28
	وقى، يقي	و ق ي	waqaa, yaqii	I, defective (as mashaa, yamshii) 27–28
prove	دلّ، يدلّ	د ل ل	dalla, yadull	I, doubled (as radda, yarudd) 31
publish	نشر، ينشر	ن ش ر	nashara, yanshur	I, regular 13–17
pull	شدّ، يشدّ	ش د د	shadda, yashidd	I, doubled (as radda, yarudd) 31
push	دفع، يدفع	د ف ع	dafaعa, yadfaع	I, regular 13–17

Read this way ———————➤

English	Arabic verb	Root	Transliteration	Verb Type	Page Reference
put	وضع، يضع	و ض ع	waDaعa, yaDaع	I, assimilated	(as waSala, yaSil) 21–22
put on (clothes, etc.)	ارتدى، يرتدي	ر د ي	irtadaa, yartadii	VIII, defective	(as ishtaraa, yashtarii) 60

Q

quake	اقشعرّ، يقشعرّ	ر ع ش ق	iqshaعarra, yaqshaعirr	IV, quadriliteral	98
quarrel	جادل، يجادل	ج د ل	jaadala, yajaadil	III, regular	(as saabaqa, yusaabiq) 42–43
question	ساءل، يسائل	س ء ل	saa'ala, yusaa'il	III, hamzated	45

R

race	سابق، يسابق	س ب ق	saabaqa, yusaabiq	III, regular	42–43
raise	ربّى، يربّي	ر ب و	rabbaa, yurabbii	II, defective	45
raise (lift up)	رفع، يرفع	ر ف ع	rafaعa, yarfaع	I, regular	13–17
reach	بلغ، يبلغ	ب ل غ	balagha, yablugh	I, regular	13–17
read	قرأ، يقرأ	ق ر ء	qara'a, yaqra'	I, hamzated	35–36
read: be read	انقرأ، ينقرئ	ق ر ء	inqara'a, yanqari'	VII, hamzated	60
receive (guests, etc.)	استقبل، يستقبل	ق ب ل	istaqbala, yastaqbil	X, regular	(as istaعlama, yastaعlim) 57–58
record	سجّل، يسجّل	س ج ل	sajjala, yusajjil	II, regular	(as darrasa, yudarris) 42–43
red: turn red	احمرّ، يحمرّ	ح م ر	iHmarra, yaHmarr	IX, regular	54
refresh	أنعش، ينعش	ن ع ش	'anعasha, yunعish	IV, regular	(as 'aعlama, yuعlim) 42–43
refuse	رفض، يرفض	ر ف ض	rafaDa, yarfuD	I, regular	13–17
regret	أسف، يأسف	ء س ف	'asifa, ya'saf	I, hamzated	(as 'akhadha, ya'khudh) 35-36
relax	استراح، يستريح	ر و ح	istaraaHa, yastariiH	X, hollow	(as istaqaala, yastaqiil) 60
remain	بقي، يبقى	ب ق ي	baqiya, yabqaa	I, defective	(as nasiya, yansaa) 27–28
remember	تذكّر، يتذكّر	ذ ك ر	tadhakkara, yatadhakkar	V, regular	49–50
remind	ذكّر، يذكّر	ذ ك ر	dhakkara, yudhakkir	II, regular	(as darrasa, yudarris) 42–43
remove	أخرج، يخرج	خ ر ج	'akhraja, yukhrij	IV, regular	(as 'aعlama, yuعlim) 42–43
rent	استأجر، يستأجر	ر ج ء	ista'jara, yasta'jir	X, hamzated	60
	أجّر، يؤجّر	ر ج ء	'ajjara, yu'ajjir	II, hamzated	(as aththara, yu'aththir) 45
repair	صلّح، يصلّح	ص ل ح	SallaHa, yuSalliH	II, regular	(as darrasa, yudarris) 42–43
	أصلح، يصلح	ص ل ح	'aSlaHa, yuSliH	IV, regular	(as 'aعlama, yuعlim) 42–43

Read this way ————————➤

English	Arabic verb	Root	Transliteration	Verb Type	Page Reference
repeat	كرّر، يكرّر	ك ر ر	karrara, yukarrir	*II, doubled*	(as raddada, yuraddid) 45
	ردّد، يردّد	ر د د	raddada, yuraddid	*II, doubled*	45
reply	ردّ، يردّ	ر د د	radda, yarudd	*I, doubled*	31
request	رجا، يرجو	ر ج و	rajaa, yarjuu	*I, defective*	(as shakaa, yashkuu) 27–28
	طلب، يطلب	ط ل ب	Talaba, yaTlub	*I, regular*	13–17
reserve	حجز، يحجز	ح ج ز	Hajaza, yaHjiz	*I, regular*	13–17
resign	استقال، يستقيل	ق ي ل	istaqaala, yastaqiil	*X, hollow*	60
respect	احترم، يحترم	ح ر م	iHtarama, yaHtarim	*VIII, regular*	(as iqtaraba, yaqtarib) 57–58
rest	استراح، يستريح	ر و ح	istaraaHa, yastariiH	*X, hollow*	(as istaqaala, yastaqiil) 60
return	عاد، يعود	ع و د	عaada, yaعuud	*I, hollow*	(as zaara, yazuur) 23–25
	رجع، يرجع	ر ج ع	rajaعa, yarjaع	*I, regular*	13–17
reward	كافأ، يكافئ	ك ف ء	kaafa'a, yukaafi'	*III, hamzated*	45
ride	ركب، يركب	ر ك ب	rakiba, yarkab	*I, regular*	13–17
rise	ارتفع، يرتفع	ر ف ع	irtafaعa, yartafiع	*VIII, regular*	(as iqtaraba, yaqtarib) 57–58
roll	دحرج، يدحرج	د ح ر ج	daHraja, yudaHrij	*I, quadriliteral*	97
run	جرى، يجري	ج ر ي	jaraa, yajrii	*I, defective*	(as mashaa, yamshii) 27–28

S

sad (be)	ابتأس، يبتئس	ب ء س	ibta'asa, yabta'is	*VIII, hamzated*	60
save (money, etc.)	ادّخر، يدّخر	د خ ر	iddakhara, yaddakhir	*VIII, irregular*	55
say	قال، يقول	ق و ل	qaala, yaquul	*I, hollow*	(as zaara, yazuur) 23–25
search	بحث، يبحث	ب ح ث	baHatha, yabHath	*I, regular*	13–17
	فتّش، يفتّش	ف ت ش	fattasha, yufattish	*II, regular*	(as darrasa, yudarris) 42–43
season (food)	تبّل، يتبّل	ت ب ل	tabbala, yutabbil	*II, regular*	(as darrasa, yudarris) 42–43
see	رأى، يرى	ر ء ي	ra'aa, yaraa	*I, defective, hamzated*	100
seem	بدا، يبدو	ب د و	badaa, yabduu	*I, defective*	(as shakaa, yashkuu) 27–28
sell	باع، يبيع	ب ي ع	baaعa, yabiiع	*I, hollow*	(as Taara, yaTiir) 23–25
send	أرسل، يرسل	ر س ل	'arsala, yursil	*IV, regular*	(as 'aعlama, yuعlim) 42–43
set off (something)	أطلق، يطلق	ط ل ق	'aTlaqa, yaTliq	*IV, regular*	(as 'aعlama, yuعlim) 42–43
share (in)	شارك، يشارك	ش ر ك	shaaraka, yushaarik	*III, regular*	(as saabaqa, yusaabiq) 42–43

Read this way ━━━━━━▶

English	Arabic verb	Root	Transliteration	Verb Type	Page Reference
shop, go shopping	تسوّق، يتسوّق	س و ق	tasawwaqa, yatasawwaq	*V, hollow*	(as talawwana, yatalawwan) 52
shorten	اختصر، يختصر	خ ص ر	ikhtaSara, yakhtaSir	*VIII, regular*	(as iqtaraba, yaqtarib) 57–58
shout	صاح، يصيح	ص ي ح	SaaHa, yaSiiH	*I, hollow*	(as Taara, yaTiir) 23–25
show	عرض، يعرض	ع ر ض	عaraDa, yaعriD	*I, regular*	13–17
shudder	اقشعرّ، يقشعرّ	ر ع ش ق	iqshaعarra, yaqshaعirr	*IV, quadriliteral*	98
shut	قفل، يقفل	ق ف ل	qafala, yaqfil	*I, regular*	13–17
sign	وقّع، يوقّع	و ق ع	waqqaعa, yuwaqqiع	*II, assimilated*	(as waSSala, yuwaSSil) 45
sing	غنّى، يغنّي	غ ن ي	ghannaa, yughannii	*II, defective*	(as rabbaa, yurabbii) 45
sit	جلس، يجلس	ج ل س	jalasa, yajlis	*I, regular*	13–17
sleep	نام، ينام	ن و م	naama, yanaam	*I, hollow*	23–25
slow (be)	بطؤ، يبطؤ	ب ط ء	baTu'a, yabTu'	*I, hamzated*	35-36
smash	كسّر، يكسّر	ك س ر	kassara, yukassir	*II, regular*	(as darrasa, yudarris) 42–43
smell	شمّ، يشمّ	ش م م	shamma, yashumm	*I, doubled*	(as radda, yarudd) 31
smile	ابتسم، يبتسم	ب س م	ibtasama, yabtasim	*VIII, regular*	(as iqtaraba, yaqtarib) 57–58
smoke	دخّن، يدخّن	د خ ن	dakhkhana, yudakhkhin	*II, regular*	(as darrasa, yudarris) 42–43
speak	تحدّث، يتحدّث	ح د ث	taHaddatha, yataHaddath	*V, regular*	(as tadhakkara, yatadhakkar) 49–50
stand	وقف، يقف	و ق ف	waqafa, yaqif	*I, assimilated*	(as waSala, yaSil) 21–22
stay (remain)	بقي، يبقى	ب ق ي	baqiya, yabqaa	*I, defective*	(as nasiya, yansaa) 27–28
steal	سرق، يسرق	س ر ق	saraqa, yasraq	*I, regular*	13–17
stop	توقّف، يتوقّف	و ق ف	tawaqqafa, yatawaqqaf	*V, assimilated*	(tawaqqaعa, yatawaqqaعa) 52
	وقف، يقف	و ق ف	waqafa, yaqif	*I, assimilated*	(as waSala, yaSil) 21–22
stop (desist)	امتنع، يمتنع	م ن ع	imtanaعa, yamtaniع	*VIII, regular*	(as iqtaraba, yaqtarib) 57–58
stop (someone)	استوقف، يستوقف	و ق ف	istawqafa, yastawqif	*X, assimilated*	60
store	ادّخر، يدّخر	د خ ر	iddakhara, yaddakhir	*VIII, irregular*	55
strengthen	شدّ، يشدّ	ش د د	shadda, yashidd	*I, doubled*	(as radda, yarudd) 31
stretch	مدّ، يمدّ	م د د	madda, yamudd	*I, doubled*	(as radda, yarudd) 31
strive	سعى، يسعى	س ع ي	saعiya, yasعaa	*I, defective*	(as nasiya, yansaa) 27–28
study	درس، يدرس	د ر س	darasa, yadrus	*I, regular*	13–17
	ذاكر، يذاكر	ذ ك ر	dhaakara, yudhaakir	*III, regular*	(as saabaqa, yusaabiq) 42–43

Read this way ⟶

English	Arabic verb	Root	Transliteration	Verb Type	Page Reference
succeed	نجح، ينجح	ن ج ح	najaHa, yanjaH	I, regular	13–17
suitable (be)	لاءم، يلائم	ل ء م	laa'ama, yulaa'im	III, hamzated	(as saa'ala, yusaa'il) 45
summon	دعا، يدعو	د ع و	daعaa, yadعuu	I, defective	(as shakaa, yashkuu) 27–28
suspect	شكّ، يشكّ	ش ك ك	shakka, yashukk	I, doubled	(as radda, yarudd) 31
swallow	بلع، يبلع	ب ل ع	balaعa, yablaع	I, regular	13–17
sweep	كنس، يكنس	ك ن س	kanasa, yaknus	I, regular	13–17
swim	سبح، يسبح	س ب ح	sabaHa, yasbaH	I, regular	13–17

T

English	Arabic verb	Root	Transliteration	Verb Type	Page Reference
take	أخذ، يأخذ	ذ خ ء	'akhadha, ya'khudh	I, hamzated	35-36
take off	أقلع، يقلع	ق ل ع	'aqlaعa, yuqliع	IV, regular	(as 'aعlama, yuعlim) 42–43
take out	أخرج، يخرج	خ ر ج	'akhraja, yukhrij	IV, regular	(as 'aعlama, yuعlim) 42–43
talk	تحدّث، يتحدّث	ح د ث	taHaddatha, yataHaddath	V, regular	(as tadhakkara, yatadhakkar) 49–50
	تكلّم، يتكلّم	ك ل م	takallama, yatakallam	V, regular	(as tadhakkara, yatadhakkar) 49–50
talk to	حادث، يحادث	ح د ث	Haadatha, yuHaadith	III, regular	(as saabaqa, yusaabiq) 42–43
taste	ذاق، يذوق	ذ و ق	dhaaqa, yadhuuq	I, hollow	(as zaara, yazuur) 23–25
teach	علّم، يعلّم	ع ل م	عallama, yuعallim	II, regular	(as darrasa, yudarris) 42–43
	درّس، يدرّس	د ر س	darrasa, yudarris	II, regular	42–43
tear	قطع، يقطع	ق ط ع	qaTaعa, yaqTaع	I, regular	13–17
tell	قال، يقول	ق و ل	qaala, yaquul	I, hollow	(as zaara, yazuur) 23–25
	أخبر، يخبر	خ ب ر	'akhbara, yukhbir	IV, regular	(as 'aعlama, yuعlim) 42–43
thank	شكر، يشكر	ش ك ر	shakara, yashkur	I, regular	13–17
think	ظنّ، يظنّ	ظ ن ن	Zanna, yaZunn	I, doubled	(as radda, yarudd) 31
	فكّر، يفكّر	ف ك ر	fakkara, yufakkir	II, regular	(as darrasa, yudarris) 42–43
throw	رمى، يرمي	ر م ي	ramaa, yarmii	I, defective	(as mashaa, yamshii) 27–28
tidy	رتّب، يرتّب	ر ت ب	rattaba, yurattib	II, regular	(as darrasa, yudarris) 42–43
tie	عقد، يعقد	ع ق د	عaqada, yaعqid	I, regular	13–17
tire	تعب، يتعب	ت ع ب	taعiba, yatعab	I, regular	13–17
touch	لمس، يلمس	ل م س	lamasa, yalmis	I, regular	13–17
train	درّب، يدرّب	د ر ب	darraba, yudarrib	II, regular	(as darrasa, yudarris) 42–43

Read this way ———→

English	Arabic verb	Root	Transliteration	Verb Type	Page Reference
translate	ترجم، يترجم	ت ر ج م	tarjama, yutarjim	I, quadriliteral	(as daHraja, yudaHrij) 97
transport	نقل، ينقل	ن ق ل	naqala, yanqul	I, regular	13–17
travel	سافر، يسافر	س ف ر	saafara, yusaafir	III, regular	(as saabaqa, yusaabiq) 42–43
treat (deal with)	عامل، يعامل	ع م ل	عaamala, yuعaamil	III, regular	(as saabaqa, yusaabiq) 42–43
trust	وثق، يثق	و ث ق	wathaqa, yathiq	I, assimilated	(as waSala, yaSil) 21–22
try	حاول، يحاول	ح و ل	Haawala, yuHaawil	III, hollow	(as naawala, yunaawil) 45
turn	لفّ، يلفّ	ل ف ف	laffa, yaliff	I, doubled	(as radda, yarudd) 31
turn (something) around	أدير، يدير	د و ر	'adaara, yudiir	IV, hollow	(as 'araada, yuriid) 45
turn over (capsize)	انقلب، ينقلب	ق ل ب	inqalaba, yanqalib	VII, regular	57–58
turn (something) over	قلب، يقلب	ق ل ب	qalaba, yaqlib	I, regular	13–17

U

understand	فهم، يفهم	ف ه م	fahima, yafham	I, regular	13–17
use	استخدم، يستخدم	خ د م	istakhdama, yastakhdim	X, regular	(as istaعlama, yastaعlim) 57–58
utilize	استعمل، يستعمل	ع م ل	istaعmala, yastaعmil	X, regular	(as istaعlama, yastaعlim) 57–58

V

view (watch)	شاهد، يشاهد	ش ه د	shaahada, yushaahid	III, regular	(as saabaqa, yusaabiq) 42–43
visit	زار، يزور	ز و ر	zaara, yazuur	I, hollow	23–25
vote	صوّت، يصوّت	ص و ت	Sawwata, yuSawwit	II, hollow	(as khawwafa, yukhawwif) 45

W

wait	انتظر، ينتظر	ن ظ ر	intaZara, yantaZir	VIII, regular	(as iqtaraba, yaqtarib) 57–58
wake (awaken)	استيقظ، يستيقظ	ي ق ظ	istayqaZa, yastayqiZ	X, assimilated	(as istawqafa, yastawqif) 60
walk	مشى، يمشي	م ش ي	mashaa, yamshii	I, defective	27–28
wander	تجوّل، يتجوّل	ج و ل	tajawwala, yatajawwal	V, hollow	(as talawwana, yatalawwan) 52
want	أراد، يريد	ر و د	'araada, yuriid	IV, hollow	45
	شاء، يشاء	ش ي ء	shaa'a, yashaa'	I, hollow, hamzated	(as naama, yanaam) 23–25
	تمنّى، يتمنّى	م ن و	tamannaa, yatamannaa	V, defective	52
	ودّ، يودّ	و د د	wadda, yawadd	I, doubled	(as radda, yarudd) 31

Read this way ———————➤

English	Arabic verb	Root	Transliteration	Verb Type	Page Reference
wash	غسل، يغسل	غ س ل	ghasala, yaghsil	I, regular		13–17
watch (view)	شاهد، يشاهد	ش ه د	shaahada, yushaahid	III, regular	(as saabaqa, yusaabiq)	42–43
wear	لبس، يلبس	ل ب س	labisa, yalbas	I, regular		13–17
wear out	تعب، يتعب	ت ع ب	taɛiba, yatɛab	I, regular		13–17
weep	بكى، يبكي	ب ك ي	bakaa, yabkee	I, defective	(as mashaa, yamshii)	27–28
welcome	رحّب، يرحّب	ر ح ب	raHHaba, yuraHHib	II, regular	(as darrasa, yudarris)	42–43
well: do well	أحسن، يحسن	ح س ن	aHsana, yuHsin	IV, regular	(as 'aɛlama, yuɛlim)	42–43
widespread: become widespread	انتشر، ينتشر	ن ش ر	intashara, yantashir	VIII, regular	(as iqtaraba, yaqtarib)	57–58
win	كسب، يكسب	ك س ب	kasaba, yaksib	I, regular		13–17
	ربح، يربح	ر ب ح	rabaHa, yarbaH	I, regular		13–17
wind	انحنى، ينحني	ن ح و	inHanaa, yanHanii	VII, defective		60
wipe	مسح، يمسح	م س ح	masaHa, yamsaH	I, regular		13–17
wish	تمنّى، يتمنّى	م ن و	tamannaa, yatamannaa	V, defective		52
	ودّ، يودّ	و د د	wadda, yawadd	I, doubled	(as radda, yarudd)	31
withdraw	انسحب، ينسحب	س ح ب	insaHaba, yansaHib	VII, regular	(as inqalaba, yanqalib)	57–58
wonder	تساءل، يتساءل	س ء ل	tasaa'ala, yatasaa'al	VI, hamzated		52
work	عمل، يعمل	ع م ل	ɛamila, yaɛmal	I, regular		13–17
work hard	اجتهد، يجتهد	ج ه د	ijtahada, yajtahid	VIII, regular	(as iqtaraba, yaqtarib)	57–58
write	كتب، يكتب	ك ت ب	kataba, yaktub	I, regular		14–16